Sears Philosophy
as taught in
"The Books Without an If"
makes life livable here and hereafter

CORRESPONDENCE COURSE

Twelve Lessons in

Concentration and Will Power

by

F. W. Sears, M.P.

AUTHOR OF

"How to Attract Success," "Sears Psychology Lessons, Vol. I and II," "Sears Philosophy Lessons, Vol. III," "How to Give Treatments," "How to Conquer Fear," "Concentration—Its Mentology and Psychology," "Everyday Experiences," "Sears Philosophy; What it Teaches; How to Study It," "Was Jesus God or Man?" "The Three Monkeys," etc., etc.

CENTRE PUBLISHING CO.
108 & 110 WEST 34 ST.
NEW YORK

PREFACE

We should never be afraid to spend our money for anything which will benefit us.

There is plenty of money in the world and there is no reason why we should not relate with whatever amount we may want.

When we do not it is because we have used our concentration and will power *wrongly* and not because there is any lack in the supply of money.

When we try to get the best of anyone in any deal we are only beating ourself by using our concentration and will power *wrongly*.

When we do anything with the consciousness of " economizing " we are

v

simply shutting ourself away from the universal abundance of the supply of everything through the *wrong* use of our concentration and will power.

When we attempt to control others and *make* them buy our goods whether or not they want them, we are using our concentration and will power *wrongly* and no matter how much profit we may make to-day as the result, the day will come when we will lose it all and everything else we may have.

All this is the result of the Universal Law which works out the effects of causes we set in motion through the wrong use of our concentration and will power.

We may say " I don't believe such rot," but that doesn't in any way affect its truth.

The time was, and not so very long

ago either, when the most intellectual men in the world did not believe such "rot" as that the world was round, and they proved conclusively (to their own satisfaction) that it couldn't be round or else the water would all fall off of it.

The best educated men of that day, as well as the Christian religion, taught also that the sun revolved around the earth and ostracised and excommunicated those who did not profess similar beliefs, but that did not make the earth square neither did it make the sun revolve around the earth.

"Ignorance of the law excuses no one," so say our civil and criminal courts," and this is in full accord with the Universal Laws; our "beliefs," no matter what they may be, do not in any way excuse our ignorance.

It is evident that you wanted to learn something you did not know otherwise you would not have purchased these lessons.

The first thing for a *real student* to do is to become *receptive to his teacher*.

This does not mean that he has to become *acceptive* and swallow everything whole at one gulp without regard to whether or not it appeals to his reason, logic and common-sense, but it does mean that he should become *receptive*, and that when he finds something which does not agree with his preconceived ideas he should not reject it at once as being untrue but he should go to work to see how well he can prove its truth to himself.

There is nothing in these lessons but what the Author *knows* is true because he has proven them for himself and has taught thousands of his students how to prove them during the past few years.

There are two ways in which to learn any lesson: One way is to memorize the words. This is the method usually adopted by most students.

The other way is to learn by absorption. That is, read the lesson over quietly, carefully, calmly, while in a relaxed condition and so absorb it rather than attempt to memorize it.

When we memorize a lesson we only get the form, the words; we get little or nothing of either their consciousness or vibration.

Memorizing a thing gives us an intellectual knowledge of it, its theory, but gives us little or nothing of its wisdom or understanding.

When we absorb a lesson we may not at first be able to express our conception of it as intellectually as it is written but we at least get the soul of it, the wisdom and understanding of it, because we *feel it* and *live it* in our consciousness.

This is the true method of obtaining wisdom and understanding, and it is the method the Author would most earnestly recommend in the study of these lessons.

The Author has no desire to force these lessons on any student, and so upon receipt of One Dollar the Publishers will mail a copy of this Preface and the first lesson to anyone who wants to examine them before purchasing the complete set.

Should the contents of these not satisfy the purchaser that they are *worth the full price of the course of lessons alone* he may return them to the Publishers any time within ten days and they will gladly refund the One Dollar.

The entire course of lessons is *not* sent out on approval for should the purchaser be satisfied with this Preface and the first lesson we *know* he will more than appreciate those which follow and that the course of study will be invaluable to him and that money could never purchase from him that which they teach.

This course of study will prove to be the turning point for constructive success in the life of each student that applies and lives its lessons.

My best wishes are always with you.

THE AUTHOR.

SPECIAL INSTRUCTIONS TO STUDENTS

After having studied the first Lesson at least half an hour each day for a week in the manner recommended in the Preface, then write out your answers to the questions, relating to that lesson, on a separate sheet of paper and without referring to the Lesson.

After you have done this then lay the Lesson and your answers aside until the next day when you will first go over the Lesson and then go over your answers and see whether or not you wish to make any changes in the latter.

When you have your answers satisfactory to you without referring to the Lesson, then copy them on a new sheet of paper and send them in to us for review by Dr. Sears.

In sending in your answers to us it is not necessary to write out the questions.

Just head the sheet of paper like this: *Answers to Questions in Lesson One.*

Then place the figure 1 at extreme left of line and follow it with the answer to question one.

When that is completed then write the figure 2 at the extreme left of the next line and follow with the answer to question two.

Continue to do this with each one of the ten questions.

The number you place at the extreme left will show us which question you are answering.

Follow these instructions in answering the questions for each Lesson.

Should there be any questions about any Lesson you would like to ask please write them on a separate sheet of paper and enclose with your letter.

Address all such letters to the

CENTRE PUBLISHING CO.,

108 AND 110 W. 34TH ST.,

NEW YORK.

CONCENTRATION AND WILL POWER

by F. W. SEARS, M.P.

First Lesson

The power of concentration when *rightly* used is man's greatest asset, but when *wrongly* used become his greatest liability.

In order to understand just what is meant by the words " rightly " and " wrongly " as used in the " Sears Philosophy " let me say that " rightly " means harmoniously or under the Law of Harmony, and that " wrongly " means inharmoniously or under the Law of Force.

Heretofore man has always been taught by those who discussed this subject, whether as a writer or teacher, that all it was necessary for him to do was to acquire a strong power of concentration and the world and everything in it he wanted would be his.

That with such a power of concentration he could *make* anything come to him he wanted.

The result of such teaching has been that man's entire work was devoted to acquiring the power to concentrate first and then directing that power towards some one thing for as long a period as he might desire.

Numerous *methods* for acquiring this power of concentration have been given, the idea seeming to be with each teacher that it was the *method* which was *the important thing.*

No attention whatever has been given to the *principles* underlying man's use of the power of concentration nor to the *consciousness* with which it was used, and the will power which manipulated it.

It is in this fact there is found the *first difference* between the "Sears Philosophy" and all other teachings.

Methods are unimportant as they are purely accessories, and any method a student finds helpful to his particular state of consciousness is good for him no matter how bad it may be for others.

When a student adopts a method which is destructive and inharmonious in his life the day comes when he realizes this truth and so learns that " the cure of a thing is in the thing itself." His experience then becomes " good " to him.

Man's *consciousness* is created by his *thought habits,* and these in turn are the result of the thoughts he thinks, not for a day or two, but for years.

There are only two kinds of *consciousness*; harmonious and inharmonious.

The former is the effect of man's use of the Law of Harmonious Attraction in his life and results in increasing, up-building and developing him along constructive lines.

The latter is the result of his use of the Law of Force (mental as well as physical) and disintegrates and destroys while *seeming* to upbuild.

The action of both of these Laws is so subtle, and the relationship between cause and effect so difficult to see objectively in many cases that unless man has developed a good perception and is a close analyst he fails to see and understand.

Every thought man thinks is either

constructive or destructive and adds to one while taking from the other of these two kinds of consciousness, harmonious or inharmonious.

Through man's will power he is able to control the kind of thoughts he thinks and therefore determine whether he will make his *consciousness and thought habits* more harmonious or more inharmonious.

No one can control this for him. He must do the work for himself. When anyone else does control his thoughts it is because he has given his power of self control to some one or some thing outside of himself.

Few persons lack the power to concentrate.

Most persons use this power ignorantly and therefore destructively the larger portion of the time.

What is Concentration?

It is the ability to fix the human mind on some one thought, idea, image, vision, thing, to the exclusion of all else.

The length of time one concentrates on anything is a factor of the will power, *not* of concentration itself.

There are many different kinds of concentration and many different methods of using this power.

One of the most common methods taught, and which many mistake as being *the only real method*, is that which is called " going into the Silence."

Under this method the student is taught, in a general way, to fix his mind on some one thought or thing and hold it there for a period of time; then let go, take his mind off of everything so that he may become receptive to that for which he has concentrated, and remain in this receptive condition for a period of time.

This method is taken from the Eastern philosophies which are taught by the Hindoos and other occultists.

In its finality this method is one of the most destructive possible to imagine, no matter how " high " and " unselfish " the thought may be on which one has concentrated nor how " holy " the object of the concentration may be before " going into the Silence."

The giving up of the control of the human mind to any mind or consciousness manifesting through some other form, even though it may be to what the world calls God himself, or to any of the lesser " Masters," no matter how " good " the object of such control may be, weakens the power of the human mind to exercise its own will in just the degree that one gives up such control, and when this is continued and persisted in for any length of time there is only one result and that is astralization, obsession, or both.

In all my experience and observation as a teacher I have never found anyone who practiced " going into the Silence " for any length of time but who became abnormal, weak-willed, and more or less unreliable as the result of it.

To become astralized is to have fastened upon one a disembodied entity; i.e., a soul which has laid down its physical body at death and is on the astral plane, which is the plane where we all go to at death.

The astral plane is made of material very much finer than is that of the physical plane. It lies all around and within the physical, the two planes interpenetrating each other.

Any condition of astralization devitalizes the physical body through the sapping of its life energy much the same as a bloodsucker or leech does. The effect is that of an invisible vampire.

To be obsessed is to have an astral entity control the human mind. This control may be either in part or in whole; periodically or continuously. In the latter event the person would be insane.

All nervous diseases of every kind and nature are the effect of astralization or obsession.

This is why the medical practitioners find it so difficult to " cure " nervous diseases.

The patient, while under the influence

of the astralizing or obsessing entity, cannot control his own mind and his power of concentration is used destructively by the controlling entity.

Every one, even though he may be insane—unless he is an imbecile—concentrates on something with his human mind during his waking hours.

There is never a moment when one's human mind is absolutely a blank.

The human mind only becomes what we call a " blank " when we cease to exercise our human will power in controlling what shall fill it.

Man's trouble is *not* that he lacks the power to concentrate but rather that he uses this power so ignorantly, unconsciously and destructively that he sets causes in motion which weaken his will power and so makes it exceedingly difficult for him to concentrate on what he wants.

We have no difficulty in concentrating indefinitely either on what interests us or that which worries and annoys us.

Our trouble begins when we attempt to *make* ourselves concentrate along lines which are out of our beaten tracks and which require a change in our habits of thought to accomplish.

All this is the result of our having used the Law of Force in developing our power of concentration and so weakened our will power that it will not respond to our continued attempt to force or *make* it follow our instructions.

Our brain goes to sleep as did that of the disciples of Jesus in the Garden of Gethsemane.

Our own troubles are of vital importance to us and so we unconsciously revive and revitalize them and the causes which produced them by our continually thinking of and concentrating upon them.

By referring to Matthew, Chapter 26, verses 36 to 45, we may read the story of Jesus in the Garden of Gethsemane and from it learn how he concentrated on sorrow.

It says that he " began to be sorrowful and very heavy." He said to the disciples who were with him, "My soul is exceedingly sorrowful, even unto death."

It says also that he prayed, saying, " O my Father if it be possible let this cup pass from me: nevertheless not as I will but as thou."

He prayed a second time saying: " O my Father if this cup may not pass away from me, except I drink it, thy will be done."

Also that he prayed a third time, saying the same words.

From this history we can see how he not only concentrated upon his troubles but also that he gave up the control of his will power to some personality outside of himself which the world has called " God."

The religionist has considered this a highly laudable thing to do. Whether or not you believe this to be so, the fact still remains that to do so weakens one's will power and makes him subservient to some power exercised by some personality other than his own.

Having taught the law and its universal application, our business is not to attempt to force the student to comply with it but to permit him to use as much or as little of it as each one may desire.

The student may well ask as to why one who knew the power of concentration as well as the man Jesus must have known it would have used it so destructively as he did in Gethsemene.

It is a truth that no one ever lives up to his highest ideals all of the time.

To do so would be to cease to grow. Stagnation and then death is always the result when the growth of anything ceases.

The man Jesus was no exception to the rule, as one can readily understand who reads the history of him in the New Testament.

As fast as we master one ideal through the constructive use of our power of concentration a still greater one comes into our vision, no matter whether these ideals are of money, health, love, strength, courage, power, harmony, or anything else.

Questions for First Lesson

1. What is the most important thing to you in this Lesson?
2. What is meant by the *right* and *wrong* use of our power of concentration?
3. What is meant by " methods? "
4. What is meant by your " consciousness? "
5. Into how many classes may thoughts be divided?   Name them.
6. What faculty of the human mind controls one's thoughts?
7. What is the difference between concentration and will power?
8. What is the destructive feature of " going into the Silence? "
9. What is its ultimate effect?
10. Why does our power of concentration faii us at times?

CONCENTRATION AND WILL POWER
by F. W. SEARS, M.P.

Second Lesson

Again let me repeat that the *character of the thoughts we think*, not just for a day or two but for months and years, determines the kind of *thought habits* we create, and that our *thought habits* in turn create the *consciousness* which underlies all of our subsequent thoughts and actions.

This *consciousness* colors every thought which comes to us and makes it more harmonious or less so, according to whether the *consciousness* itself is harmonious or inharmonious.

According to the biblical history of

17

Jesus he allowed human sympathy to control him many times, and he indulged in anger, "righteous indignation," condemnation, criticism, on several different occasions.

All of these thoughts and emotions had their effect on the *thought habits* he formed and the *consciousness* underlying them.

They all helped to make for a consciousness of inharmony which, when he allowed his human mind to concentrate on sorrow in Gethsemene, overpowered him, slowed down his vibrations, as evidenced by the statement that he " began to be sorrowful and very heavy," and quickly precipitated him into the currents where it was possible for the crucifixion to follow.

We see the same thing worked out in every day life when we learn to study and analyze life from all planes of consciousness, free from bigotry, prejudice and dogmatism.

A case came under my notice once of a man who had been very proud of his good name, reputation, business and financial ability.

He was exceedingly sensitive for and proud of the standing in his community which these things gave him, and, like the granite rock in one of Ella Wheeler Wilcox's poems, " He gazed on the world and was satisfied."

He had place, power, wealth, health, and every *thing* which the material world could give to make him happy.

Then suddenly he was arrested one day on a charge of embezzlement. It was very quickly shown that there was not the slightest grounds for the accusation, and that the charge had been made by a person who was irresponsible in every way, had no financial standing and had been used as a political tool in the matter.

The man was quickly released and the charge dismissed with an apology.

The destructive effects of the wrong (inharmonious) use of his power of concentration had begun to materialize in this man's life.

He commenced to lose his pride and, unconscious of what he was doing and the effects which would result, concentrated upon his disgrace at being charged with such a crime even though he knew he was innocent and his innocence had been shown to the world.

As the result of his continuing to live in and concentrate upon these destructive thoughts his health began to fail and he had an exceedingly severe illness.

In addition to this he failed in business, lost everything he had and was left badly in debt.

A little later on family troubles began to creep in and to crown all of the destructive harvest of the wrong (inharmonious) use of Energy by his power of concentration being centered on pride and resentment at the seeming injustice of man, he discovered that his wife was unfaithful to him and not only had several lovers but had seduced his oldest son by a former marriage.

With his good name tarnished, his pride shattered, his health, money and family honor sacrificed by the woman he adored, he was again like the granite rock which, " All unwarned, with a mighty shock, out of the mountain was wrenched the rock. Bruised and battered and broken in heart, it was carried away to the common mart, wrecked and ruined in peace and pride. ' Oh, God is cruel,' the granite cried, ' Comrade of mountains, of stars the friend; by all deserted; how sad my end.' "

It was about this time that he came to me for consultation not knowing which way to turn nor what to do.

Every old landmark upon which he had depended in the past had been shattered.

Every ideal, which he had ignorantly and unconsciously transformed into idols, had been broken.

There was absolutely nothing left upon which he could lean for support nor from which he could derive any consolation in his great hour of need.

Love, money, health, friends, courage, strength, hope, faith, all had left him as the result of his inharmonious use of his power of concentration.

The great tragedy of it all was, not only with him but with every life which finds itself in a similar condition, that he did not know he had caused it all himself by the inharmonious use of his power of concentration.

He did not know that the universal Energy he had used ignorantly and unconsciously to destroy him could be used to restore him to health, wealth, love, strength, peace, power, courage, hope, faith.

But it can be so used when one learns how to use his power of concentration *rightly*, constructively and harmoniously.

I took him under my personal care; showed him how he had set all the destructive causes in motion himself which had produced all of these inharmonious effects, and that he did it through the *wrong* use of his power of concentration when he allowed his thoughts to dwell on anger, hatred, worry, fear, anxiety, condemnation, criticism, envy, jealousy, pride, resentment, resistance, and kindred thoughts and emotions.

As the result of applying the Sears Philosophy to the living out of his daily life he gradually began to regain his health, strength, courage, ambition, self-respect.

Life commenced to take on an entirely new aspect for him and to-day he is happy, contented and doing a great work for mankind in his chosen profession.

The last verse of the poem referred to well describes the final result of the

application of the Sears Philosophy to
this man's life.

A dreaming sculptor, in passing by,
gazed at the work with thoughtful eye.
Then, stirred with a purpose supremely
grand, he bade his dream in the rock
expand. And lo! from the broken and
shapeless mass that grieved and doubted,
it came to pass that a glorious statue
of priceless worth and infinite beauty
adorned the earth."

The artist described in this poem had
devoted his life to concentrating on the
ideal, the good, and saw it in the granite
rock.

He was not blinded by the rough and
ragged exterior of the rock but looked
back of and beyond its outward form and
saw the glorious beauty which was locked
up within.

So with this man when he came to me for consultation. I saw a great soul within which was neither vile nor vicious, but which was simply ignorant of the constructive and harmonious use of his power of concentration.

I *knew* that when this power was *rightly* used it would rebuild him in all the glory and grandeur and greatness of the God or good which is always within each life.

We are all more or less familiar with our physical body but what the world generally does not know is that we have an astral body, a thought body, as well as still other bodies which are made of yet finer and finer material.

Next to the material or physical body comes the astral, and then the thought body.

Each of these bodies is made in the same general shape and form as is the physical body but of finer material, just as the clothes on our physical body are made to conform with its shape and contour.

The thought body interpenetrates the astral, and the astral body interpenetrates the physical.

Each of these bodies has a brain the same as has the physical body through which it functions.

Thoughts cut channels and raise ridges in the thought body, and these are in turn impressed on the astral body which, in turn, impresses them on the physical body, just as the physical body impresses them on our outer clothing.

The ridges and bumps on the physical head by which phrenologists are able to determine one's characteristics are formed in this manner.

Each thought, however, is like a drop of water in the mighty ocean and it takes many of them to form a channel or build a ridge.

Each thought, word, or symbol of any kind has its own particular vibration of atoms which causes it to be *different* from all others.

While this is true it is *not* the words, thoughts or symbols themselves which are wholly responsible for the kind of channels cut but it is the feeling, the *consciousness and thought habit*, back of them which has the stronger influence and controls.

Both are very important and have a determining effect on the kind of channels formed.

Words and thoughts have power according to the vibrations they symbolize, but these vibrations may be either accentuated or entirely annulled by the character and quality of the *consciousness* with which they are used.

We see the truth of this statement in the world's diplomacy where words with a double meaning are used frequently.

We can also take any word such as " hate " or " kindness " and either increase its power or take it away entirely by the *consciousness*, the feeling, we put back of its use.

The channels and ridges which are formed and persist are the result of the *thought habits* formed by the same character of thought being repeated many times.

Thus the vibrations of all harmonious thoughts—no matter what the specific

words may be—are of the same character,
viz.: harmonious.

All inharmonious thoughts are also of
the same character but differ materially
in their character from the harmonious
ones.

The *thought habits* formed, as indicated
by the channels and ridges, produces
the *consciousness* which underlies future
thoughts and actions.

We want to remember that there are
only two kinds of *consciousness*:—harmonious and inharmonious.

Every thought we think, every word
whether spoken or unspoken, belongs
to one or the other of these two kinds of
consciousness.

Each one adds to or takes from one or
the other of these two kinds of *consciousness.*

When it rains the water that falls is pure but some of it falls in the ocean and becomes salty; some falls in impure and stagnant water and so partakes of that quality; some falls in a mud puddle and becomes impregnated with its impurities; while some falls in pure water and so remains pure.

Questions for Second Lesson

1. What is the most important thing to you in this Lesson?
2. What does " character of thought " mean?
3. What effect does " sorrow," " regret," and similar thoughts have upon the " character of thought? "
4. What effect does concentrating on the " wrong " character of thoughts have upon both the physical body and our environment?
5. What is one of the greatest tragedies of life?
6. What relationship do thoughts of anger, worry, fear, sorrow, regret, and similar thoughts and emotions have to success or failure?
7. What will the power of concentration do for each life when it is used *rightly*?
8. What do thoughts do to the thought, astral and physical bodies?
9. Which is the most powerful—the vibrations of the thought itself or that of the consciousness back of them?
10. How is one's consciousness created?

CONCENTRATION AND WILL POWER

by F. W. SEARS, M.P.

Third Lesson

The kind of water into which the rain falls determines whether or not the rain remains pure.

So with the thoughts which come to us from time to time. The state of *consciousness* back of our *thought habits* determines whether the thought will be harmonious or inharmonious in its effect.

It is because of this latter fact that so many find it very difficult to get anything but inharmony when they first attempt to use their power of concentration on some very harmonious affirmation.

Their *consciousness and thought habit*

33

is so inharmonious that the harmonious vibrations of the words used in the affirmation are not strong enough to make any kind of an impression or lift one out of the inharmonious currents with which he is related.

The only effect a harmonious affirmation has in such cases is to cause irritation, annoyance and so arouse greater inharmony.

It requires the greatest kind of persistency, continuity, and the utmost patience in making the affirmations in such cases before even a ray of harmony begins to enter the human mind.

In one case which came under my notice the student worked most faithfully for more than six months without any feeling of harmony coming to him.

Most persons would have grown tired

of the attempt and quit but he had the *real want*, and while he was discouraged at times yet he believed he was on the right track and so kept everlastingly at it.

After a careful examination and study of his case I found that his trouble laid in the fact he was so deadly in earnest that he used his power of concentration in making his affirmations in a strained and tense condition.

His very tenseness shut him away from the vibrations of the words he was affirming and made it impossible for him to receive them.

After teaching him how to relax and let go, allowing him to become receptive while he was affirming, it was not long before he began to *feel* their harmonious relationship.

Gradually he began to change his

thought habits, and they in turn created the new *consciousness* of harmony.

In relaxing and becoming receptive to the vibrations set in motion by the making of an affirmation the student must be especially careful in continuing to use his power of concentration in holding to the affirmation, keeping his human mind *filled* with it to the exclusion of all else.

This is necessary in order that he may not fall into the dangerous habit of " going into the Silence."

Should his mind wander to some other thought during these periods of concentration then bring it back again to the affirmation without any irritation, annoyance, condemnation nor self-accusation, but do it gently and kindly.

It is only by bringing the human mind

back to the affirmation gently and kindly, i.e., harmoniously, that one finally succeeds in becoming the complete master of his thought world under the Law of Harmony.

The line of demarkation between doing the work constructively and destructively is very close here and the student must train his will power to hold the affirmation continuously to the exclusion of all other thoughts but this work of training must be done without strain, effort or tenseness or it later on becomes very destructive.

There are many different kinds of concentration all of which react and have their effect on the individual just to the extent one does not use his will power harmoniously in the control and use of his power of construction.

There is first the concentration of the individual.   Then comes that of the family, race, city, state, nation.

There is also the concentration of the social, political, business, professional and religious worlds with their multitude of clubs, societies and other organizations too numerous to mention.

As the result of the collective concentration of the individual along political lines we have the political parties and the various officials or rulers of City, State, Nation, Empire.

The character of such officers symbolizes the level of the consciousness of the people they represent or rule.

As the result of the collective concentration of the individual along other lines we have the various religious sects; the social caste and classes; the various kinds of business, finance, professions, arts, educational institutions, etc.

Each group, sect and class symbolize the level of the consciousness along its particular line of the people composing it.

In all of these different classes there are various degrees of development and unfoldment in the individuals composing them, from the least to the greatest and back again, but the average, the level, of the consciousness of each division is to be found in its ruler or the " authority " which controls it, and the laws, rules and regulations which are enacted for its government and guidance.

Before it is possible to change any condition of the individual, city, state, nation, or race, whether such changed condition is to be in the physical body or the environment, the *consciousness and thought habit* of the individual must be changed.

The work must be done on and by the individual, the unit, and as it progresses in the individual so will it progress in the city, state, nation or race.

The Roman Catholic Church is frequently quoted as saying that " When it can have the child under its care and training during its early years it has no fear of its ' backsliding ' in the future."

This is because it has realized that the *consciousness and thought habits* formed in youth require a large amount of *right concentration* to change any time later in life and that the *majority* of persons are too ignorant and mentally lazy to do the work on themselves which it is necessary to do in order to effect any change.

The individual is the foundation, the starting point, the unit, on which the continuance or change of any *consciousness and thought habit* is based for it is *the individual, through his human mind, that has supreme power here in the material world.*

Few persons will recognize the wonderful truth of this statement even when their attention is especially called to it.

Soulfully ignorant man is too prone to belittle his supreme power while intellectually developed physical and mental man is too prone to aggrandize his personality and personal power.

Neither one recognizes the existence of the greater power and finer methods possessed by and inherent to the soul in every life.

The individual must be educated and

developed in the constructive and harmonious use of this power of concentration as a soul power, not simply as a mental or physical force, before any of the much to be desired " reforms " can ever be permanently established.

He must get away from the idea of considering the soul and its power from the so-called religious viewpoint which has beclouded his vision in the past and learn to look at it as he would his physical and mental faculties, *knowing* that just as his mentality is only a finer method of manipulating physical laws, so is his soul a still finer method than his mentality which is to be used by him in the manipulating of these same physical laws.

The *wrong* or destructive use of this power of concentration has always resulted in religious and political wars among people, nations, and races and these will continue, with only brief intermissions, as long as man continues to use his power of concentration *wrongly*.

While it is impossible for a people, a nation, or a race, as a whole, to escape the destructive effects of its *wrong* use of the power of concentration yet the individual can *rise above* their destructive effects in so far as he is personally concerned through the *right use* of his power of concentration, and as " a little leaven leavens the whole loaf," so will the *consciousness and thought habit* of the people, race and nation be gradually changed through the increasing number of individuals who make the change in their own life and the influence of the harmonious atmosphere which emanates from them.

One of the most destructive uses to which man puts his power of concentration is found in his desire to ".convert" the rest of mankind to his particular line of thought.

This is one method which man in the ignorant aggrandizement of his personal self and his lack of deeper understanding uses with such disastrous effect both to himself and the one who is forced to be "converted" through his fear and ofttimes against his own consciousness of reason and common-sense.

There is only one person in the world whom we ever need to "convert" and that is our own self.

It is all right to *teach* others whenever they are ready and willing to be taught but to in any way attempt to *make* them believe, or to have a consciousness back of our teachings which would in any manner *want to force them to accept* any teaching, no matter how " good " it might be, is most destructive both to the teacher and the one who allows himself to be so controlled.

This is one reason why my books are always sold under the guarantee of " your money back unless perfectly satisfied."

Under no circumstances should we attempt to force the "Sears Philosophy" upon any life.

Every soul that is ready to accept its teachings and to whom its lessons would be of benefit will never need to have it *forced* upon him, and all others would not find in it that which would be for their highest, best and greatest good.

Each life has all eternity in which to learn its lessons and it has a perfect right to take all of the time it wants, and to learn them in any manner and by any method it desires, and we should learn not to attempt to hurry it along any faster than it *wants* to travel.

In addition to the wars which come as the effect of the causes set in motion by the *wrong* use of man's power of concentration collectively expressed, we have the diseased, crippled, deformed physical bodies, and the criminal, poverty-stricken environments into which the individual souls are born and to which others not so born migrate during an incarnation for the same reason, that is as the effect of the causes they have set in motion, ignorantly and unconsciously it is true but none the less surely, as the result of their *wrong* use of their power of concentration in this and former incarnations.

Sorrow, misery, pain, suffering, despair, sickness, disease, injury, accidents, shame, degradation, poverty and lack of all kinds will continue for the individual, race, state, nation, as long as man continues to set the causes in motion which produce these effects through the *wrong* use of his power of concentration.

How do we use this power of concentration *wrongly* so that it results in such destructive effects?

Questions for Third Lesson

1. What was the most important thing to you in this Lesson?
2. What effect does one's consciousness have on the thoughts which come to him?
3. What frequently prevents the vibrations of an affirmation from reaching us? and what should be done under such conditions?
4. What will prevent the student from forming the dangerous habit of " going into the Silence? "
5. When the mind wanders during concentration what should be done; how should it be done, and why?
6. What does the character of collective concentration along any line symbolize, and to what extent does it affect the individual?
7. What is the first step to take in order to change any condition of the physical body or environment, and who only can do this?
8. Why does the Roman Catholic Church seldom lose those who are brought up in its faith?
9. What faculty of man has supreme power in establishing and controlling all his relations here in the material world?
10. What is one of the most destructive uses to which man can put his power of concentration?

CONCENTRATION AND WILL POWER

by F. W. Sears, M.P.

Fourth Lesson

By creating the inharmonious *consciousness* from the *thought habits* which result from living in and concentrating upon any kind of an inharmonious and destructive thought or emotion such as anger, hatred, fear, worry, anxiety, sorrow, misery, remorse, righteous indignation, self-pity, unhappiness of any kind, condemnation, criticism, resentment, resistance, envy, jealousy, impatience, intolerance, bigotry, human sympathy, strain, effort, tenseness, and all the other multitude of inharmonious thoughts and emotions.

49

In the story of Gethsemane we are told that " Jesus began to be sorrowful and *very heavy.*"

To become " very heavy " means that one's vibrations have slowed down to a point way below normal.

Our relationship to such slow vibrating currents being abnormal we can only find in them that which makes for sorrow, misery and all the discords of life.

It is not necessarily the things we relate with while in such currents but it is the attitude we take to them which makes their effect on us while in such currents, discordant and inharmonious.

While in such currents we become melancholy and are filled with fear.

Our deeper understanding leaves us; our belief is destroyed; our faith is lost and our hope dies out.   We become the prey to all the discordant and inharmonious forces of the universe.

It is while in such currents that man frequently rails at and curses God and his fellow man; that he commits deeds of desperation and sometimes takes his own life; these are only some of the things he relates with there.

At the garden of Gethsemane the man Jesus said to his disciples: "My soul is exceedingly sorrowful, even unto death."

With such use of his power of concentration *wrongly* it is not at all strange that the crucifixion followed shortly thereafter.

His death was not the result of some prophecy foretold centuries before, preordained and finally consummated as a vicarious atonement for the sins of others.

It came solely as the result of his *wrong* use of his power of concentration and his failure to *rise above* its destructive effects.

Physical death never occurs except as the result of the violation of some law of the physical plane, and until we learn to *rise above* the effects of such laws through the *right* use of our power of concentration physical death will continue to occur in each life solely as the natural and normal effect of such violations.

According to the biblical history of Jesus' ministry his power of concentration was so strong and its action so free and responsive that he was able to materialize things almost instantly.

As evidence of this fact we have the story of the turning water into wine which was accomplished by changing the vibrations of the atoms of water to correspond with those of wine.

The materializing of the two pieces of silver in the fish's mouth; the calming of the waves in the storm; the feeding of the multitude, and the numerous cases of healing the body of its diseases, sickness, deformities, obsessions, etc., were all instances of the changing of the vibrations of the atoms towards which he directed his power of concentration.

A concentration which can send its thought out into the formless Energy everywhere around us and materialize the silver in the fish's mouth without the atoms having to go through the slower process of their natural evolution which brings them into the mineral kingdom under normal law;

A concentration which can again reach

out into this same formless Energy and
materialize bread and fishes with which
to feed the multitude without these
things having to go through the slower
process of their normal evolution;

A concentration strong enough to im-
press its thought on the atoms of the water
in the waves of the sea and calm them in a
storm;

A concentration which can stamp its
thought on the intelligence in the atoms
of water and change their vibrations to
that of wine;

A concentration which is obeyed by the
intelligence of every atom in the human
body, changing its inharmonious relationship with the rest of the body to that
of harmony and thus producing health
where sickness had persisted;

A concentration which can speak to

the intelligence in the atoms of disembodied entitles on the astral plane which
have been obsessing the human body,
causing them to let go their hold thereon
and allow the inflicted person to become
normal and well;

A concentration powerful enough to
be obeyed by the intelligence of every
atom towards which it is directed, whether
it be of the mineral, the vegetable, the
animal or the human kingdom and change
their harmony or inharmony as each case
requires, is certainly strong and powerful
enough to set causes in motion in a very
few minutes, when not *rightly* used, to
destroy and disintegrate its physical body
or cause its crucifixion.

Men and women all over the world
with a far lesser developed power of
concentration have destroyed their physi-

cal body and caused its death at every stage of the world's existence.

Another destructive and *wrong* use of his power of concentration is shown when in this same Gethsemane Jesus said: "Not my will but thy will be done," and he emphasized this through repetition several times.

In the past, through our ignorance of the great Universal Laws and the *right* use of the power of concentration, we have been taught it was a high and holy thing to bow our heads to the will of some one or some thing which was supposed to be superior to us, whether such superior being was a God, a King, an Emperor, or some greater "authority."

Our will power is given us to exercise here in the external world of people and things so that we may use all of our faculties to the highest, best and greatest that is within us.

How can man ever learn to use his faculties in this way *unless he does use them?*

We can be taught all there is about writing for instance; how to form each letter perfectly; how to make the curve and straight line of each letter in the most symmetrical manner possible but unless we *use* this knowledge and keep applying it through persistent practice with pen or pencil we will never learn to write even though we completely memorize all the principles of penmanship.

So with our will power.

Man will never learn to develop his will power to a point where he can use it in exercising his power of concentration constructively or *rightly* unless he *uses* his will power continuously and so gives it the exercise necessary to make it strong.

When man gives up his will, even to the being he calls God, he is doing a most destructive thing for he is putting himself under the power and control of something he considers is outside of, separate and distinct from himself.

As long as man depends on some power outside of himself for support and guidance he is a leaner and just so long will he fail to use his power of concentration *rightly* at the critical moments of his life and so he will continue to reap the destructive effects of the causes he has set in motion, such registration being made either in his body or environment, or both.

Jesus said: " A prophet is not without

honor save in his own country and in
his own home."

That statement, which is true to-day
the same as it was two thousand years
ago, tells the story of another way in
which man uses his power of concentration *wrongly*.

As the result of man's inharmonious
consciousness and the *thought habits* which
produced it, his first impulse is generally
to see the faults, weaknesses and imper-
fections in every person and every
thing.

Man's whole training has been to find
the defects. He is taught to " Never
mind the good points but to keep a sharp
watch for the weak ones."

In the handling of things this training
is supposed to be necessary in order to
prevent any work which is imperfect or

in any way deficient from being approved.

In his relationship with people he has been taught this training is necessary in order to protect him from the bad, the wicked, the vile and vicious, so that he may not be contaminated by associating with them.

The result has been to train man to concentrate on the weak points, the ignorant and imperfect results, rather than upon the *consciousness and thought habits* back of them and which could just as easily produce the perfect results was it properly trained to do so.

When man learns to concentrate first on the good or God within himself and then upon the good or God within every other life, *knowing* that all life is one in its finality and that as he lifts himself up into these more harmonious currents so will he aid in the lifting up of all the rest of mankind, he will then gradually begin to attract to him manifestations of Energy, both in body and environment, which will become more and more perfect as he himself becomes more and more perfect in thus using his power of concentration *rightly.*

Man will then become a prophet of harmony through using his power of concentration *rightly* and will cease to attract to him the inharmonious expressions of those of his own country and home but will receive from them the great recognition which only a *harmonious consciousness* can attract.

" Can any good come out of Nazareth? " was asked when it was said that Jesus came from there.

This question is still another illustration of the power of concentration used *wrongly*.

Nazareth was in " bad " repute simply because the Jews continued to live in and concentrate on that which gave it a " bad " reputation rather than upon that which would give it a " good " reputation.

They simply refused to think or believe it was possible from its reputation for anything " good " to come from there and so it continued to remain impossible to them.

They were like a man who came to me one day and said he was a failure in life and did not know what to do.

I asked him how long he had been a " failure."

All his life, he said.

I told him he must have enjoyed it immensely seeing how long he had held on to the fact that he was a failure.

He said he didn't like it.

I then asked him why he didn't quit being a failure.

He said he could not help it. He had tried to but did not succeed.

I told him that his trouble was that he had only " tried " and that all of his attempts had been made externally and with the consciousness of failure.

Questions for Fourth Lesson

1. What is the most important thing to you in this Lesson?
2. How do we create an inharmonious *consciousness and thought habit?*
3. What is the effect of relating with abnormally slow vibrating currents through the thoughts we think?
4. How may physical death be postponed indefinitely?
5. How did the man Jesus perform the so-called miracle of turning water into wine?
6. How did the man Jesus use his power of concentration *wrongly* in the Garden of Gethsemene?
7. Why is it destructive to depend on some power outside of the Universal Power which manifests in every one's soul?
8. Why is a " prophet not without honor save in his own country and in his own home? "
9. Why is it destructive to train one's self to see and concentrate upon the weak or " bad " points in people and things instead of upon the strong or " good " points?
10. What makes " reputation? "

CONCENTRATION AND WILL POWER

by F. W. SEARS, M.P.

Fifth Lesson

The place to begin to quit being a failure is in the *consciousness and thought habit.*

That is the place to begin to quit being anything and everything we do not want.

It is also the place to begin to be everything and anything we do want.

The law works both ways.   Which way it does work is dependent entirely on how we use our power of concentration.

This man had been a *failure all his life,* according to his own story.

Why?

Simply because all his life he had ignorantly and unconsciously · used his
power of concentration *wrongly*, and in
later years had only added to *his success
as a failure* by concentrating upon the
thought that he was a failure, in addition to the many other ways in which he
continued to use his power of concentration *wrongly*.

I taught him to realize that he was
to-day born anew.

That the old life, with all its destructive
consciousness and thought habits of inharmony and its ignorant use of his power
of concentration, was dead and buried
and that this was a new life upon which
he was just entering, a new day, a new
time.

That the past had ceased to exist for
him and that in his new birth he had

risen above all the old failures and in-harmonies of the past.

That whenever his mind did revert back to the past he was to refuse to allow it to dwell there but was to live in the ever present *now* and concentrate upon the thought that he was the very biggest kind of a success *now*.

He was to continue exercising his will power and concentration on thoughts and ideas which would upbuild and create the kind of *consciousness and thought habit* he wanted.

He was to use the same common-sense method in doing this that he would use in learning to play the piano, or as he did use when he learned to read and write.

He was to practice doing this each day, devoting as much time to it as he could, and that did he devote one-half as much time to following these instructions as he had been devoting to using his power of concentration *wrongly* that it would not take any time from his daily duties and would enable him to turn a lifetime of failure into an evening of the greatest success.

He went to work with himself and through the *right* use of his power of concentration he built an entirely new *consciousness and thought habit* of harmony which resulted in making him very successful not only in a financial way but also in rebuilding his body into perfect health, and attracting friends in both the business and social worlds which brought him the greatest happiness.

This man transformed his life from one of unhappiness and complete failure to one of joy, happiness and great success in a few short years through learning to use his power of concentration *rightly*.

Another man came to me once who had met with financial reverses and who found it impossible, so he said, to find employment as no one wanted "old men."

He was a fine accountant and had the executive ability and experience to manage an office yet everywhere he went he was met with the statement that they "did not want old men."

He did not realize that his *wrong* use of his power of concentration in the past had set the causes in motion which registered as financial loss in his case, and that after this loss had occurred his concentrating on his misfortune and living in the inharmonies of that kind of a consciousness continued to set other causes in motion by which he was led only to such places as did not want " old men," and that by being constantly met with this kind of a reply he had increased his *wrong* use of his power of concentration by adding to it the thought and affirmation that it was impossible for an " old man " to obtain a position.

He was sure of the truth of this for he had demonstrated its truth over and over again beyond any question of a doubt and neither I nor anyone else could ever make him believe it was not true.

He had never realized the great truth which is that we can demonstrate and prove anything we want.

That the real question of life is " What do we *want* to prove? "

We can " prove " that we are a success or a failure.

We can " prove " that " old men " cannot get a position of any kind, or we can " prove " that they can.

We can " prove " that we are sick with an incurable disease, or we can " prove " that our disease is curable and get well.

We can " prove " that all women are flirts, inconstant and vampires and that all men are thieves, scoundrels and roués, or we can " prove " that all men and women are high-minded, honest, straightforward and good.

Which do we *want* to prove?

The real answer to our question determines how we will use our power of *concentration* and the kind of *consciousness and thought habit* we will create.

These two things will determine the

kind of relationships with people and things we will establish and enable us to "prove" either side of any proposition.

I informed this man that I had no desire to *make* him believe anything.

My work was that of a teacher and it did not make any difference to me whether he believed what I taught or not.

That in my work as a teacher I never attempted to "convert" anyone and would not lift a finger to make him believe any of the Sears Philosophy.

That I was perfectly willing to allow him to retain all his old ideas and beliefs just as long as he wanted to do so.

That I was also perfectly willing to allow him to continue reaping the inharmonious and destructive effects of his old causes, his old thoughts, ideas and beliefs, just as long as he wanted to do so.

That it had long since been demonstrated to me as a truth that the majority of mankind never learned any real good commonsense until they were good and ready to do so and that I had no desire to waste my time and energy in attempting to hurry up the process in any particular individual who was not yet ready to learn.

That my time could only be had by those persons who were ready to learn and who wanted to learn with a want sufficiently strong and powerful to be willing to do the work on themselves which it was necessary to do in order to learn.

There is an old adage which says that: " The cure of a thing is in the thing itself," and this is true.

The only way some persons will ever

learn to be constructive is to be so destructive first that they carry themselves
down into the very depths of misery,
sickness, poverty and despair, and then
in the anguish and pain of their suffering are their eyes opened to their own
creative power and their responsibility
for its constructive use by their power
of concentration.

I told this " old man " that as long as
he was *sure* an " old man " could not get
a position just so long would he continue
to " prove " that it was impossible for
him to obtain one.

The reason he would " prove " it was
impossible for him to obtain a position
was that his *wrong* use of his power of
concentration would continue to lead
him only to such places as did not want
" old men."

There were plenty of positions, I told him, where " old men " were employed and where age, ability and experience, such as he had, were considered an asset instead of a liability but that by the *wrong* use of his power of concentration he had set such causes in motion as made it impossible for him to be led by the law of his life to such places.

That had he created a *consciousness and thought habit of harmony* and then concentrated on the thought of its being possible for him to obtain a good position only one-tenth as much as he had been concentrating on the thought of its being impossible, he would have long since made the connection.

The world has yet to learn that what it calls " facts " are only materialized thoughts, and that the wildest and apparently most impossible dreams of the imagination can become "facts" in the due process of time will we only use our power of concentration *rightly* and so build the kind of a *consciousness and thought habit* which will materialize them.

The length of time it will take for us to do this will depend wholly upon how persistently and harmoniously we do our work.

I told this man he should *fill* his imagination with the thought that there were plenty of good positions ready and waiting for "old men" and that one of them was ready and waiting for him to get sufficiently harmonious and receptive to relate with it.

He should allow his soul, his God-self or good-self, to inspire him with this belief and then use his human mind to hold this thought, displacing all others as fast as they came to him which might in any way tend to impair or destroy this one.

That by concentrating on this thought or idea continuously and persistently whenever he could think to do so he would begin to create a *consciousness and thought habit* which would attract the kind of a place he wanted and which wanted him just as much.

That by *attracting* it to him under the Law of Harmony, as he would do by following these instructions, he would be able to hold it as long as he wanted to do so.

He followed these instructions faithfully and it was not long before he obtained a position which, while not all he had desired, gave him a fair living.

He continued to work with himself to create a still more harmonious and constructive *consciousness and thought habit* with the result that he gradually continued to improve his condition until he was doing far better as an "old man" than he had ever done before in his life.

Since my original book entitled "Concentration—Its Mentology and Psychology" was published there have been Employment Agencies established in some cities, so I have been informed, which make a specialty of obtaining positions for "old men."

Similar results occur in the life of many persons because of their unconscious concentration on the thought of "I can't," or "I'll try."

More persons become failures through

the *consciousness and·thought habit* they create as the result of such thoughts than the world imagines.

These two little phrases are more deadly to the soul than is the most virulent poison to the body.

The world, however, loves to use them so much that no vocabulary seems to be complete without them.

Were it possible for words to wear out from constant use it is certain that " I can't," and " I'll try," would have been worn threadbare centuries ago.

Questions for Fifth Lesson

1. What is the most important thing to you in this Lesson?
2. Where is the first place to begin to quit being a failure and become a success?
3. Why are we successful in becoming and remaining failures, and what is it necessary to do to transmute failure into success?
4. When our mind reverts back to past failures what are we to do?
5. How are we led to relate with people and things we do *not* want, and how can we relate with those we do want?
6. How do we create the kind of a *consciousness and thought habit* we want?
7 How can we " prove " anything we want to prove?
8. What is the only way some persons will ever learn how to use their faculties constructively?
9. Why did the " old man " finally find a place where " old men " were wanted?
10. What are two of the most common and destructive phrases man uses, and why are they destructive?

CONCENTRATION AND WILL POWER
by F. W. Sears, M.P.

Sixth Lesson

We have been taught in the past that " I'll try " was a good attitude or state of consciousness to have.

When we analyze the consciousness which is usually back of it we find that it is no better than " I can't."

When we have the " I can't " consciousness we admit failure right at the start.

When we have the " I'll try " consciousness it implies the possibility of success but carries with it, back behind the implied possibility of success, the recognition of the stronger probability of failure.

81

This action is so subtle that we do not realize what a handicap to the possibility of our success it is and therein lies its great danger.

During the Spanish-American war the commanding General called one of his officers and instructed him to capture a post held by the enemy.

The officer recognized it was a difficult task, one that was considered almost impossible with the force at his command, and so said, " I'll try."

The General looked at him and said, " You will not do."

The officer then said, " I'll do the best I can."

The General replied, " You will not do."

The officer then said, " I'll take it."

The General replied, " Go."

The General knew the difficulties which would be met in the attempt and he knew that nothing less than the positive statement of " I'll take it " would succeed.

Several years ago a boy of sixteen started out for himself to make his way in the world.

His first position was at $5 a week. While filling that he obtained one of my books on " Concentration—Its Mentology and Psychology " and determined to put into practical application the lessons taught therein.

The result was that in a little over two years he had risen to a position where his salary was $38 a week.

A woman came to me once to obtain help for her husband who " was getting dull and stupid," so she said.

When they were first married she

began to call him " stupid " whenever
he did anything she did not like and had
continued to do this ever since and now
it seemed to her as though he really was
" getting stupid."

She had never realized that by concentrating her thought on the word
" stupid," even though she had done it
unconsciously and without any " bad "
intention, and continually bringing before
him an image and thought of stupidity,
she was holding up before him a pattern
which, while he did not have to accept it,
yet the intelligence in his brain cells
would copy and reproduce unless he was
strong enough to and did refuse to give
such an image and thought any power
over him.

Few persons are strong enough to do
this, and we all know that the " constant

dripping of water will in time wear away the hardest stone."

Another woman came to me with the complaint that her husband was so careless and disorderly in his habits that her home was a most unhappy place.

She was an exceedingly orderly person who wanted everything " just so " and worked herself and her servants almost to death in attempting to maintain her standards.

The building of a consciousness of law and order about the home and everything else is a good thing, a much to be desired accomplishment, but to do this under the Law of Inharmony is only another way of using our power of concentration *wrongly*.

We only get that which we create for ourselves by the use we make of our power of concentration.

This woman did not realize that through the inharmonious *consciousness and thought habit* she had created by the *wrong* use of her power of concentration she had related with a man for a husband whose consciousness was as disorderly as hers was orderly.

She did not realize that it was her continued *wrong* use of her power of concentration which made her home unhappy and caused her to permit her husband's carelessness to have such power over her.

She did not know that these conditions could never be corrected by her continuing to use her power of concentration in creating and maintaining her inharmonious *consciousness and thought habits.*

The first thing she was to do was to stop attempting to " reform " him and go to work " reforming " herself by creating a *consciousness and thought habit* of harmony.

She was to recognize that her husband had just as good a right to be careless and disorderly as she had to be careful and orderly, and that when she recognized that right and refused to become disturbed or inharmonious about it one of two things would occur; either he would gradually cease to be disorderly or else she would be taken out of that kind of environment and placed in one which better accorded with her new and harmonious *consciousness and thought habits.*

She was to concentrate on the thought of " All is good " every time her husband's carelessness or any other inharmonious thought came to her.

Make this affirmation over and over as

fast as she could and thousands of times a day.

Sometimes in the beginning this might be a purely mechanical action as the old *consciousness and thought habit* of inharmony was too strong for the vibrations of " All is good " to have much effect, but that by continuing to affirm it because she *wanted* to do so and not because she made herself do so, this attitude would gradually grow stronger and more powerful, increasing both the action of her will power and the power of her concentration until she ceased to feel any mechanical action in her affirming.

She went to work upon herself faithfully to create this new *consciousness and thought habit* of harmony and by using her power of concentration *rightly*

in accordance with these instructions, she
changed her whole life.

She became more kind, pleasant and
agreeable (so much so that her friends
marveled at the great change) her husband gradually ceased to be so careless
and disorderly and began to confine
what was left of his disorderly habits
to his own private room.

The wife began to express herself
through her music (she had a wonderful
voice and was a fine pianist besides)
and made most marvelous advancement
as the result of her increased harmony.

To round out the good work the husband and wife, after having lived for
years in a sort of armed neutrality, began
to again enjoy each other's companion-
ship and all because the wife had done all
her " reform " work upon herself, ceased

to " make over " her husband by force, and began to set the causes in motion herself which would attract from him that which she so much desired—a harmonious relationship between them.

Now you husbands are not to get " all puffed up " as the result of this incident because none of these good results were at all due to any conscious or intended action on the part of the husband but were due entirely to the intelligent and conscious action on the part of the wife in learning how to use her power of concentration *rightly*.

By such *right* use of her power of concentration she ceased to set the causes in motion which attracted from her husband the kind of an atmosphere and actions which made her home inharmonious.

Those conditions, and the ability to express them, still remained in her husband's consciousness and until he works with himself to create a harmonious *consciousness and thought habit* they will remain there ready to manifest at any moment should the wife lapse back into her old *consciousness and thought habit of inharmony.*

The wife attracted these more harmonious expressions from her husband solely as the result of using her power of concentration *rightly* as I had taught her to do.

One of the most pitiful and yet most interesting cases which ever came to me was that of a woman who was "in society."

She had one of the best developed and most cultivated intellects it has been my good fortune to contact.

She was bright, witty, cutting, sarcastic, with a repartee which was all the more deadly because it was so subtle.

She was a leader by birth, education, development and inheritance; possessed of an ability far beyond the average, yet she was only able to retain her leadership among those who craved the favors she was able to grant because of her position and so were afraid to cross her will.

The result was that her ambition had been thwarted on a number of different occasions, her spirit broken, and she a nervous wreck when she ran across one of my books and came to me as the result.

Her whole trouble was that she had used her power of concentration *wrongly*; that is she had used it to *force* things, to *make* people and things do her bidding instead of using it to *attract* them to her.

It is a universal law that " we can only *retain* a thing by the same law under which we *obtain* it."

When we obtain a thing under the Law of Force we must be prepared to use our force against all comers all of the time or else we go down before the greater force.

Again the more we use force in our life the greater becomes our destructive power in its reaction upon ourselves when the time comes for us to reap the harvest of the seed we have sown and the reaction sets in.

There is never any action without its corresponding reaction, and the reaction from our use of force is sure and certain, and is most destructive in its effect upon our body, environment or both.

I taught her how to create a *consciousness and thought habit* of harmony through affirming and *filling* her thought world with harmonious and constructive thoughts like " All is good," and similar ones; concentrating on them and living in the vibrations of the currents with which such thoughts related one.

She was to exercise her will power by refusing to live in the consciousness or thought of anything which made for inharmony.

I told her it was not at all necessary for her to cease being bright or witty, but it was necessary for her to change the *consciousness and thought habit* of inharmony back of her witticisms which her sarcasm had created, to one which was free from all such thoughts and emotions and contained only the greatest tolerance and kindness.

This in time would create the new

consciousness and thought habit of harmony which was so necessary in her life and which would lift her above all the currents which made for inharmony both in her body and environment and which had brought about her nervous condition and defeated her ambition.

She was under my care for some time in the training and upbuilding of this new *consciousness and thought habit* of harmony with the result that she was fully restored to health, again took up her activities in society and became one of the most successful leaders.

All of this came about as the result of using her power of concentration *rightly* and *attracting* to her that which she desired instead of *forcing* it to come to her as she had always done before.

Questions for Sixth Lesson

1. What is the most important thing to you in this Lesson?
2. Why is "I'll try" a weak and dangerous statement?
3. What is the effect of the constant affirmation of and concentration upon any thought?
4. Why are two persons of opposite tastes and habits frequently found in the same family? and what is the first thing to do in such cases?
5. Who is the only person that ever needs "reforming" and why?
6. When affirming "All is good" seems to be mechanical in its action, how may such mechanical effect be eliminated?
7. When we do all our "reform" work upon ourselves and cease attempting to "make over" others, what is the effect and why?
8. How did the "woman in society" use her power of concentration *wrongly*?
9. What is the Universal Law under which we are able to retain things?
10. When we obtain a thing under the Law of Force how long can we retain it?

CONCENTRATION AND WILL POWER

by F. W. SEARS, M.P.

Seventh Lesson

One day a young woman violinist came to me who had an aggravated case of self-consciousness.

She had no trouble in playing beautifully when she was alone, she said, but the moment she appeared before an audience, when composed even of her most intimate friends, her ability to play seemed to leave her with the result that her playing was only common and ordinary.

Her trouble was fear resulting from her self-consciousness which was occasioned by her thinking of and concentrating too much upon herself instead of upon the wonderful harmony of the spheres with which she could relate and reproduce upon her violin.

I told her the first thing she was to do was to learn to forget herself in the larger subject of her music.

She was to remember only that she was simply a vehicle through which by the proper use of Energy harmoniously directed by her power of concentration, could be produced the most marvelous and awe inspiring melodies imaginable.

It was not she, the personal self, which did this any more than it was she that made an automobile run. She, the personal self, simply directed where and how the automobile should run, and that this same thing occurred in the production of the music.

It was not her personal self which created the music but it was *through* the personal self that the music was expressed and that when she repressed this personal self by continually directing her power of concentration towards it, it was impossible for the personal self to express and so it had to do the only other thing it could do and that was to repress.

I instructed her that in order to be able to forget her personal self she was to direct her power of concentration on the thought and affirmation of " All is good " every moment she could spare.

She was also to play in public at every opportunity she could get no matter how much she was bothered by her old trouble, but that each time she played in public she was to spend from one-half to one hour in the seclusion of her dressing-room and all this time to concentrate on and affirm " All is good."

She was not to think about her music or anything else but just to keep concentrating upon and affirming " All is good."

She was to be sure and pay no attention to results; that is, whether or not she was improving but was to keep on doing this right along without regard to results; doing it because it was the highest, best and greatest thing she knew how to do.

When we do anything because it is the highest, best and greatest thing we know how to do, we do it as a matter of principle and it becomes a part of our character which strengthens it, but when we do anything for the results it brings, we do it as a matter of policy and it weakens our character.

We always want to remember that while making this affirmation of " All is good," and similar ones, ʌe should relax, let go, and become receptive to the currents with which the vibrations of these affirmations will relate us.

The more we become able to do this the better will we absorb the harmony with which they will relate us.

I told her that as she grew this new *consciousness and thought habit* of harmony so would she express her increased harmony in her playing.

The reason we should pay no attention to results is that the very thought of looking for results implies a consciousness of doubt, fear and worry that the results may not be forthcoming.

This is using our power of concentration *wrongly* for it directs Energy towards the inharmonious currents and so retards our progress in the growing of our new *consciousness and thought habit* of harmony.

This young woman had the *real want* and she went to work with herself in a thoroughly honest and conscientious manner with the result that in a month's time she began to show considerable improvement and in the course of a year's time she went from a player of mediocre ability to that of a master.

She had the ability in her already developed but not until she had changed her old *consciousness and thought habit* of inharmony to that of one of harmony was she able to *express* this great ability.

The great trouble with the world everywhere, in music, art, literature, in the business and professional worlds, in so-

ciety, in science, philosophy and religion,
is the Law of Force—mental power—
used in the belief that this is the greatest
law there is.

And so it is the greatest law of the
physical and mental planes of consciousness.

But there are planes of consciousness,
and finer methods to be used, beyond
the physical and mental planes and with
which man can relate here and now,
which so far transcend these two lesser
planes, that man as yet has not begun to
realize his wonderful possibilities.

To understand this Law of Force and
its manipulation by the power of concentration with man's mental faculties
is what the schools, colleges and universities of the world teach as "psychology."

It is no more *real psychology* than black is white.

Just as black is the absence of all color while white is the harmonious union of all color, so is the " psychology " of the schools, colleges and universities of the world the absence of all *real psychology* because such teachings are limited only to the physical and mental planes.

Real psychology is the union of all planes of consciousness manifesting in one perfect and harmonious whole, under the Law of Harmony.

The Law of Force is the opposite manifestation of the Law of Harmonious Attraction.

While the *words* which are used to manipulate both of these expressions of the law may be exactly the same, the *consciousness and thought habit back of the words are entirely different*, and herein lies the great secret.

It is this difference between the *consciousness and thought habit* back of the words used which is so difficult and almost impossible for those on the physical and mental planes of consciousness to understand.

It is this difference between the *consciousness and thought habit* back of the words used which causes those who are still functioning largely on the physical and mental planes of consciousness to depend so much on the words, the form, the rules and regulations, the conventionalities of life, the creed, dogma and ceremonies of its science, its philosophy and its religion.

It is the absence of the *consciousness and thought habit* of harmony back of its teachings that empties the Churches of the world and made the Church impotent and powerless in the great world war.

Here and there some minister or priest has unconsciously grown this *consciousness and thought habit* somewhere down the line of his cosmic journey and *rises above* the limitations of the creed and dogma of his Church.

Such men always wield an influence and power for good in their community unknown elsewhere among others in their profession.

A young man came into our office one day looking for work, and said he had tramped the streets of New York for six weeks but could not find a position anywhere.

I asked him why he did not go to the

places where they wanted to employ men instead of wasting his time and energy in coming to those that, like ourselves, did not need any more help.

He looked at me in astonishment as though he either did not understand what I said or else thought I was making fun of him.

He had never considered the matter in that light and was too inharmonious to do so even then.

He was a bright, intelligent young fellow, quite a bit above the average, but he was one of those persons who had used his power of concentration *wrongly* in former incarnations and so is born into this one with a *consciousness and thought habit* of inharmony which manifests in a grouch of some kind most of the time.

He had come to the City with the idea

vaguely formed that he was going to step right into a good position the day of his arrival.

There was nothing the matter with this idea; it was simply his *consciousness and thought habit* back of it which was all wrong as the result of his *wrong* use of his power of concentration.

Had this idea been formed with a *consciousness and thought habit* of harmony back of it and which *knew* there was a good position here waiting for him, and that the Law of Harmonious Attraction in his life would lead him to it, he would have had no difficulty in relating with it.

Instead of this kind of a consciousness created by a thought habit of harmony, he came to the City with his idea of obtaining a position backed up by a consciousness and thought habit of inharmony of which one of the principal inward manifestations was a grouchy feeling of resentment and resistance towards all the world.

Fear and anxiety were other emotions he felt and lived in, and it was in this kind of a consciousness that he started out after work.

It was no wonder he walked the streets of the City and only applied at such places as did not want his services.

There were thousands of places that did want the kind of services he could give but it was impossible for him to find them as long as he continued to use his power of concentration *wrongly*.

Had he obtained employment while continuing in such a state of conscious-ness as he was in when he came into our office he would only have used such position and the money it brought him to still further destroy himself through his *wrong* use of his power of concentration.

I took the time to talk with him for a while and showed how he had kept himself out of a position by the thought attitude he took, and how he could set new causes in motion which would relate him with a good position would he learn to use his power of concentration *rightly* as I am teaching in these lessons how to use it.

I might just as well have talked to the wind for he was not yet ready to learn his lesson of the *right* use of his power of concentration.

It was experiences of this kind which caused the man Jesus to say: " Do not cast pearls before swine."

This means that we are not to use time

and energy in attempting to " convert " anyone to these great truths who is not yet ready for them.

Each life has all eternity in which to learn its lessons and it has the right to take as long a time and have as many and varied experiences in doing so as it may desire.

There never is and never can be the power to accomplish any end or desire by the life which refuses to find that the ability to express such power lies in its own thought world through the *right* use it makes of its power of concentration.

There is always an ability to find employment, to succeed along any line, to accomplish any aim in life, no matter what it may be, for the one who first recognizes his power to accomplish, and

then uses such power in the material world
knowing he will succeed.

History is replete with incidents show-
ing the power of concentration and the
constructive and destructive results which
come from its *right* and *wrong* use.

Columbus concentrated on discovering a
north-west passage by water to India and
America was given to the civilized world.

The Huguenots concentrated on religious freedom and the Pilgrim Fathers
landed at Plymouth Rock.

Their children concentrated on political freedom and the Declaration of Inde-
pendence was signed.

Alexander concentrated for world dominion and wept when there were no
more nations to conquer.

Napoleon dreamed of a world empire
and St. Helena was the result.

Questions for Seventh Lesson

1. What is the most important thing to you in this Lesson?

2. What causes self-consciousness and how may it be cured?

3. Why should we do that which we do because it is the highest, best and greatest thing we know how to do, without regard to results?

4. When we concentrate on any thought what is necessary to do to become receptive to its vibrations?

5. What effect does " looking for results " have upon one?

6. What is the greatest law of the physical and mental planes of consciousness?

7. What do the schools, colleges and universities of the world teach as " psychology? "

8. What is *real psychology?*

9. What make the difference between " psychology " and *real psychology?*

10. What is the great Universal Law underlying *real psychology?*

CONCENTRATION AND WILL POWER

by F. W. Sears, M.P.

Eighth Lesson

Germany concentrated on being *the* world power and perfected the greatest military machine and commercial organization ever known to man.

She was rapidly subjugating the world commercially when she thought the time ripe to control it politically and the greatest war history records was begun.

With every external thing and condition in her favor at the beginning of the war,

With ample money, credit, supplies; an army vastly greater in numbers and far better trained than any other nation;

115

a navy equal or superior to that of every other nation with but one exception; with a commerce extending to every section of the globe and a fleet of merchant vessels second to none; with the power to choose when and where to strike the first blow because of her preparedness which was far in advance of every other nation;

With the power of concentration of her people for years directed " to the day " when she would strike,

With every external thing and condition in her favor when she struck the first blow,

Why did Germany not succeed in her ambition to dominate the world and enforce her Kultur on all the rest of mankind?

We find the explanation clearly and

succinctly stated in the saying attributed to the man Jesus:

" To him that hath shall be given and he shall have an abundance but to him that hath not shall be taken away even that which he hath."

Man in his purely physical and mental states of consciousness has only understood this saying from its purely objective effect, from the material manifestations of Energy, for this was all that the " psychology " of his science, his philosophy and his religion could teach him from either of those planes of consciousness.

Translated into the language of the Sears Philosophy, which gives man a larger interpretation and a deeper understanding, we would write this saying as follows:

"To him that applies the Law of Harmony in his concentration to the living out of his daily life shall be given and he shall have an abundance of everything he desires, but to him that hath not the Law of Harmony but who uses the Law of Force in his concentration in the living out of his daily life shall be taken away even that which he hath."

There are two ways in which man can use his power of concentration; one is under the Law of Harmony (the Law of Harmonious Attraction) and the other is under the Law of Force.

Under the former we do all of our work upon ourselves, that is upon our own *consciousness and thought habit*, and create such a condition of harmony therein that people and things come to us because *they want to come.*

The more work we do upon ourselves under this Law of Harmony the more powerful and attractive do we become.

The work being done upon ourselves direct it is cumulative in its effect upon us.

The people who are attracted to us and the things (money, health, love, strength, power, courage, friends, etc.) we obtain under this Law of Harmony are used by us under this same law to create still more harmony and a still greater power of harmonious attraction in our life.

This is why it is true that " To him that hath shall be given and he shall have an abundance."

The law we use and express in the living out of our daily life gives us the abundance of everything simply because we use our power of concentration *rightly* and in a harmonious relationshlp with the universal law.

We not only get the benefit of the direct action of Energy by our constructive use of our power of concentration but we also get the benefit of its reaction.

On the other hand when we work under the Law of Force our work is always directed towards the " other fellow " in our consciousness.

We attempt to control him both physically and mentally and *make* him do our bidding.

Should our will power and power of concentration not be strong enough to control him in one way we attempt it in others; we work on his fear, his cupidity, his ambition for place, power or position in the business, the financial, the political, the professional, the artistic, the social, the religious world as the case may be.

We do anything which is necessary in order to accomplish our object of *making* him obey our will.

We control him through the power of " mental suggestion," through hypnotism, through " converting " him by argument or otherwise.

Right here is where the action of the Law of Force is so subtle that it is difficult for the novice to fully appreciate or understand it.

When we " argue " a question with any one we always do so with the consciousness back of it which desires to " convert " to our way of thinking. This is using the Law of Force.

We can say exactly the same things but with a consciousness back of it which only desires to teach and does not care whether or not our statement is believed and we are *not* using the Law of Force.

The *real teacher*, the student of *true psychology*, the one who lives under the Law of Harmony and uses his power of concentration *rightly*, *knows* this greater truth and *knowing it* is perfectly willing to teach it to one who *wants* to learn it, and is just as willing to let the one who is not yet ready to learn it take all the time he wants to take in which to get ready to learn it.

He recognizes that under the Law of Force results can be obtained; that they are obtained again and again by the various methods used by those living under it; that they will continue to be obtained under this law until each life using it has had enough and is ready to learn its lesson, for

" Be not deceived; God (the great Universal Law) is not mocked; for whatsoever a man soweth, that shall he also reap," and in the fullness of time, either in this or in some future incarnation, we do reap the harvest of the seed we have sown until we learn to use our power of concentration *rightly* and so become able to *rise above* the effects of all our old ignorant and destructive causes.

Our very desire to control another's will power when persisted in has its reactionary effect on us in due time and our own will power begins to weaken and sometimes goes to pieces completely as the result.

When we direct our power of concentration towards the " other fellow " it always has to be done all over with each new case.

We fail to get the cumulative effect of our thought action on the " other fellow " because of this change in objects toward which it is directed but we do get the cumulative effect of its reaction upon ourselves.

As force was back of our thought action, force will be what we will receive from its reaction.

The law under which we obtain a thing determines the use we will make of it.

When we obtain anything (health, money, love, friends, strength, courage, place, power, etc.) under the Law of Force we are sure to use them under the same law.

It is self-evident then that the more

we get of anything and everything under the Law of Force, the more we have of it to and do use in an inharmonious and destructive manner.

With this understanding of the working out of the Law of Force we can readily see how true it is that " unto him that hath not this Law of Harmony but who uses the Law of Force shall be taken away even that which he hath."

This result does not come as a " punishment " from some God who lives in some far off heaven but it does come as the natural effect of the causes man sets in motion under the Law of Force.

A sharp knife drawn across the hand will cut it.

This result does not come as a punishment (for it will cut the hand of a " good " man just as quickly as it will

that of a "bad" one) but as the effect
of natural law.

This same thing is true with every other
effect which comes to us.

This is why when a man loses his
fortune through speculation, bad or un-
wise investments, or has it stolen from
him, he always blames the "other fellow" and claims it was "through no
fault of his."

This is why some persons have severe
sick spells, or meet with terrifying accidents and claim it was "through no
fault of theirs."

This is why we are born into families
and establish relationships with those
whom we love dearly and who have set
causes in motion in their former incarnations which causes them to be taken away
from us in their childhood, their youth,

their prime of life, or whenever we need them the most, " through no fault of theirs " we say, and *surely* " through no fault of ours."

It is because of man's ignorance and lack of understanding (not intellectual but soul ignorance) through the *wrong* use he has made of his power of concentration that these things come to him.

Instead of seeking deeply the *real cause*, which always lies within himself, he attempts to shift the blame on some one or something else, rails at and curses God, asks " Why God permits such things to occur," or else dumbly submits with a consciousness which says in effect " Oh, what's the use? "

God, the great Universal Law, permits anything to occur which comes as the effect of the causes set in motion, and nothing else ever does occur.

When we learn our lesson, which is that the remedy for all these effects we do not like lies in our power of concentration and then *apply* our knowledge, we will cease to set the causes in motion which produce the effects we do not want.

The power which controls here in the objective world is our human mind.

It is through our human mind that we create the *consciousness and thought habits* which results from the character of the thoughts we think and the use we make of our power of concentration.

Universal Law is immutable, irrevokable, unchangeable.

Man cannot destroy, annihilate nor overcome it.

But he can develop a consciousness

which will enable him to *rise above* its effects on any plane whenever he is ready to do so.

In this way does he ultimately become his own saviour and redeemer.

The ability to use our power of concentration *rightly* comes only through training and practice.

It is never a " gift," but comes only as the result of developing our ability through its constructive use.

The same is true in regard to the development and use of our will power.

Both the will power and our power of concentration can be used by the human mind under either the Law of Harmony or the Law of Force.

We can use Energy to materialize. *things* (money, health, love, strength, courage, etc.) under either law.

Questions for Eighth Lesson

1. What is the most important thing to you in this Lesson?
2. How was the collective concentration of Germany *wrongly* used?
3. What are the methods by which man may use his power of concentration? Name them.
4. State briefly the distinguishing features of these methods.
5. What is the difference between argument and teaching?
6. What determines the constructive or destructive use we make of our health, money, love, friends, courage, strength, etc.?
7. Why is it destructive to even attempt to control another's will power?
8. On whom does the cumulative effect of our thought action fall?
9. What is the supreme or controlling power in the objective world?
10. How does man obtain the ability to use his power of concentration *rightly?*

CONCENTRATION AND WILL POWER
by F. W. Sears, M.P.

Ninth Lesson

We always want to remember that the one expression of the law upbuilds and increases, and the other expression disintegrates and destroys while outwardly it is apparently *seeming* to upbuild.

This is what occurred in the German Empire, and that is why it could not win the war under the Universal Law.

The ideal of the German Empire was autocratic. All for the State. The State was supreme, the master, and the people its servants.

Only such souls incarnated in German bodies as had set the causes in motion in former incarnations which related them with this ideal.

They continued, as a people, to use their power of concentration in exercising the Law of Force to its highest degree with the result that they apparently built up an impregnable Empire.

When the war started they were apparently successful; in fact they were successful in their attacks against such nations as were built on ideals similar to their own.

When force meets force the stronger force is always sure to win, and so Belgium, Serbia, Montenegro, Russia and Roumania went down before the stronger force.

France and England were built on a greater ideal. All for the people. They were supreme, the master, and the State was their servant.

Their ideal was the Law of Harmonious Attraction and while they were not perfect in its manifestation yet it was the ideal of the people as a whole and one upon which they used their power of concentration.

As the result they brought into use in their defense a soul energy, a consciousness, which all the *force* of the German Empire and its allies was not able to master for several years, and when the time came that it seemed possible that the Law of Force manifested by the Germans might succeed the Universal Law stepped in with America.

The United States is the greatest nation in the world simply because its ideal from the date of its birth has been the Law of

Harmonious Attraction as indicated by the democracy of its Constitution.

From the moment the *soul energy* of the United States entered the war there was not the slightest chance for Germany to win for when force is pitted against harmony the former must and does go down.

And so " To him that hath the Law of Harmony in his life shall be given and he shall have an abundance but to him that hath not the Law of Harmony but who uses the Law of Force shall be taken away even that which he hath."

The man Jesus taught this great truth again when he said to his disciples at the close of his Sermon on the Mount:

" Take no thought, saying, What shall we eat? or, What shall we drink? or, Wherewithal shall we be clothed? for your Heavenly Father knoweth that ye have need of all these things. But seek ye first the kingdom of God, and his righteousness; and all these things shall be added unto you."

Translated into the language of the Sears Philosophy this would read as follows:

"Seek ye first the kingdom of good (the Law of Harmony) and its rightness, and all these things (food, drink, clothing, etc., that is every material thing) shall come to you in a perfectly harmonious manner and over perfectly normal lines of transference for the Universal Law—God—knows that ye must have all these things in abundance in order to become the most fitting instrument through which Energy may express here in the material world."

When we use our power of concentration *rightly* and live this Law of Harmony in our daily life we find that this explanation comes true both in our body and environment in just the degree we are able to and do create the *consciousness and thought habit* of harmony.

This does not mean that we have to become absolutely perfect in our manifestation of the Law of Harmony and never have a thought or expression of inharmony before its wonderful effect becomes apparent in our life.

But it does mean that we have to consecrate our life to the Law of Harmony; begin to live it each day as best we can; begin to fill our human mind with thoughts of harmony no matter what comes to us from the objective world; begin to take a harmonious and constructive attitude towards everything with which we contact; *begin to use our power of concentration rightly.*

It also means that no matter how imperfect our effort to live this Law of Harmony at first may be that we are to keep on working with ourselves to live it *knowing* that the more we earnestly practice in our work of living it the more perfect will our manifestation become.

It also means that we are to continue living it without regard to the apparent results which seem to come from our early attempts.

We are to continue living it although everything we hold dear, our good name, reputation, love, health, fame, fortune, respect of our friends and the whole world may be swept away.

We are to live this Law of Harmony as a matter of *principle*, **NOT** as a matter of *policy*.

We are to live it because it is the highest, best and greatest thing we know how to live.

We are to live it because our *want* to use our power of concentration *rightly* and so become the most harmonious and constructive vehicle through which Energy can manifest is so strong and powerful that it will not allow us to fall back into and under the power of our old Law of Force no matter what price we may have to pay in our work of transmutation.

We are to live it because we recognize the God or good within our own soul and have determined to make a perfect and complete union between our Personality and Individuality, our human and divine selves.

The writer of the first chapter of Genesis tells us that " man was created in the image or likeness of God," NOT necessarily in the shape or form but in the " image or likeness; " that is, in the *consciousness and thought habits* of God, or good, or harmony.

Also that man possesses all the great creative POWER of the Universe and can manifest it here and now in the material things of the objective world.

Man is the most developed form or vehicle here in the material world through which Energy can manifest and therefore has dominion over all the lesser forms or vehicles.

The human mind is the faculty through which man exercises or manifests this

God or good POWER, and through which he uses Energy to materialize his thought creations in the objective world according to the *right* or *wrong use* he makes of his power of concentration.

Every season the farmer has to plow and harrow his fields before he plants the seed in order to get the ground in proper shape so that the seed will take root and grow.

So with man when he wants to form new thought habits (which is his method of planting new seed and growing a new crop) he, too, has to plow and harrow the old inharmonious thought furrows in his brain.

When the human mind has been used ignorantly and destructively under the Law of Force it is necessary to fill up these old furrows of inharmony in the brain matter with new, harmonious and constructive thoughts in order to get it into proper shape for the new seed of harmony to take root and grow.

This takes time and earnest work on our part to accomplish, and many times we become faint-hearted at the apparently slow progress.

After the seed is planted we are to continue to cultivate it so that it may grow strong and powerful enough not to become overpowered by the weeds, that is the inharmonious thoughts which will come to us again and again as the result of our old and *wrong* use of our power of concentration.

Every time we allow ourselves to think of a weakness or fault *and dwell upon it* we are using our power of concentration *wrongly* for it causes us to unconsciously dig the inharmonious thought furrows deeper thus making just that much more work for us to fill them up.

On the other hand every time we think, breathe, feel and live harmonious thoughts we are using our power of concentration *rightly* for we are filling up the inharmonious thought furrows and making it just that much easier to plow the harmonious ones deeper.

It has been said that: " We are held accountable for every idle word or thought."

This is true and means that each thought has its effect for harmony or inharmony in the building of our *consciousness and thought habits*, and that the effect of each thought is in full accord with its character.

We should therefore put a conscious

watch on every thought that comes to us.

We should learn to analyze and dissect it and so learn its character, displacing at once the thoughts which tend to make for inharmony in our life with those which make for harmony.

A very good affirmation on which to center our power of concentration in such cases is: " I am harmonious NOW," also, " All is good."

We should build these vibrations into the thought furrows of our mind matter so that God, or good, our harmonious self, can manifest through them with constantly increasing strength and power.

This will enable us to get and keep in touch with the harmonious and constructive vibrations of the universe.

We should at all times be the master

of our own thought world and allow only such thoughts to remain with us as *we want*.

The power of concentrated thought produces the vibrations and creates the atmosphere which emanates from us and makes for failure or success according to their kind.

An atmosphere of failure can only produce more failure.

An atmosphere of success cannot help but to produce still greater success.

Which do we want?

We can have either.

It is just as easy to set the causes in motion which will produce success as it is those which can only produce failure.

The same energy will produce either one according to the use we make of our power of concentration.

The man who sees himself only as a physical body, a human being either with or without a soul, unconsciously concentrates on his Personality and the *power of things* in the objective world.

The result is that he lives in the consciousness of the *manifestations of Energy* uses the Law of Force with which to supply his material needs and so unconsciously separates himself from " All is good " or God.

Questions for Ninth Lesson

1. What is the most important thing to you in this Lesson?
2. What are the two expressions of the Law and how do they act?
3. Why is the United States the greatest Nation in the world?
4. What did the man Jesus mean by " Seek ye first the kingdom of God and his righteousness and all of these things shall be added unto you?"
5. How soon can we begin to improve our *consciousness and thought habits?* Do we have to wait until we are perfect?
6. Why should we live the Law of Harmony?
7. What is man's greatest possession?
8. What is the faculty through which man manipulates his power?
9. Why has man dominion here over all lesser forms?
10. What effect does our thinking and concentrating on harmonious thoughts have upon us?
11. What produces the atmosphere or vibrations which emanate from us?

CONCENTRATION AND WILL POWER
by F. W. SEARS, M.P.

Tenth Lesson

The man who sees the *oneness of all life*—NOT the oneness of all *manifestations* of life—but the oneness of the life itself which is back of all manifestation.

The man who sees that he is a part of this universal life which is manifesting in and through a human body is concentrating on his union with God or good and so sees only the good in its finality which is back of all manifestation.

Such a man *knows* that every vibration emanating from him will in due process of time return to him.

He may be a " dreamer," like the

147

sculptor, and live in his ideals, concentrating on their beautiful harmony and seeing only the perfect ideal, the perfect image, beneath the rough exterior of every granite rock, but when he *really lives* these ideals in his thought world it will not take him long to materialize them in form objectively.

That is why we teach the student to use his power of concentration and will power to hold the thought and affirm that "All is good," and thus create the harmonious *consciousness and thought habit* which sees, lives in and materializes its ideals.

The power of concentration when used *rightly* enables us to become master sculptors of our own life with our finer methods and thought tools, and we then learn to know that

" No man shall place a limit to our strength.

That triumphs such as no mortal ever gained will be ours.

That all heights not yet attained *our* feet shall tread.

And we press on, and on, and on, until we do achieve."

AFFIRMATIONS

The following affirmations are given as illustrations of constructive statements which may be used and from which we can form other affirmations of our own which may be peculiarly fitted for our particular case.

Every word and every combination of words has a vibration peculiar to itself, and symbolizes the state of consciousness of the maker thereof.

It will also symbolize that of the user whenever he makes such words his own; that is whenever he *feels* they are a part of him and he of them.

The student should always use the affirmation which gives him the greatest inspiration and the strongest feeling of power and harmony.

Sometimes an affirmation which has inspired us greatly seems to lose its power.

In all such cases we should use some other one for the time being.

Each student should practice forming a series of affirmations of his own, such as he finds on practice are best fitted for his personal use.

Before making any affirmation the student should relax, let go, and get just as receptive to its vibrations as he possibly can.

It is only by so doing that he is able to relate with the currents with which the vibrations of his affirmation will connect him and so receive their beneficial effects.

While in this relaxed condition one should never permit his mind to wander nor allow any thought, other than that he is affirming his oneness with, to enter and find lodgment in his consciousness.

This is where the danger of " going into the Silence " comes in, for to allow other thoughts to find lodgment in his consciousness at such a time will result, when persisted in, in allowing astral entities (which many persons call " angels," " Masters," " God ") to control him in time.

In order to build a *consciousness and thought habit* of harmony the student should make it a point to affirm " All is good," at every opportunity, and continue to do this as long as he lives.

We can never form such a *consciousness and thought habit* of harmony too strongly.

There will never be a time in all the ages yet to come when we will not need it.

We carry with us all down the ages the essence of the consciousness and thought habits we form on our cosmic journey.

The reason for the student affirming that he has what he .wants *now* is to create the consciousness of his union, his *oneness*, with it and so rise above his old consciousness of his separation from it which he has continued to materialize in form.

There is no time but the *Eternal Now*, for when what we call tomorrow comes it has ceased to be to-morrow and is *now*.

When one builds for the future in his consciousness, whether such future is " to-morrow or years hence as we measure time, he never catches up with it for it is always just ahead of him.

Again it is just as easy for one to

materialize what he wants to-day as it is for him to do so a year hence, provided he has the *consciousness* of his power to do so.

Affirming our *oneness* with what we want *now* builds that *consciousness* in time and makes possible our materialization.

All is good.

I am health *now*.

I am wealth *now*.

I am success *now*.

I am strength *now*.

I am courage *now*.

I am peace *now*.

I am power *now*.

I am harmony *now*.

I have an abundance of money *now*.

Wealth is manifesting for me *now*.

Happiness is filling my life *now*.

Health is stamped on every cell of my body *now*.

I am *one* with everything I desire *now*.

The things I want are mine *now* because they want me.

I am whole, strong, well, young, rich, happy and harmonious *now*.

With every breath I inhale I am attracting to me *now* that which I desire.

I am more harmonious and constructive in my *consciousness and thought habits now* than ever before.

The Peace and Harmony of God's Universe is manifesting in me *now* and I am *one* with everything I desire.

I consecrate myself to the perfect Law of Harmony. No matter how imperfect my manifestations may be at any moment, I will continue my consecration throughout all time.

My consciousness is *filled* with its union with the abundance of the supply of everything; health, wealth, love, friends, courage, strength, peace, power, harmony.

I have a good position *now* where everything is constructive and harmonious; where I am receiving a good compensation commensurate with the services I give, and where nothing but my highest, best and greatest good can come to me.

The Universal God-Energy is manifesting perfect health in me *now;* it is causing each organ of my body to perform its normal function in a perfectly natural and harmonious manner *now*; it is disintegrating and dissolving all abnormal and inharmonious cell tissue *now*, and is reviving and revitalizing my body and making it over in perfect health and harmony *now*.

The student should always remember that thoughts of worry, fear, anger, hate, anxiety, impatience, intolerance, condemnation, criticism, resentment, resistance, envy, jealousy, strife, revenge, egotism, bigotry, strain, effort, desire to " convert the other fellow " to our way of thinking (all argument is simply a desire to " convert ") are one and all negative, destructive thoughts and emotions.

WILL POWER

by F. W. Sears, M.P.

The will power is such a subtle and abstract thing apparently that it is no wonder mental man is prone to consider it so elusive and intangible a thing as to be impossible of definition or understanding by human mind.

The human mind however is capable of being trained to a point where it not only understands the physical and mental states of consciousness but also those still finer states of the soul and spiritual planes which lie beyond the mental.

Man is a composite being and consists of several different bodies each composed of the same universal substance but varying largely in the fineness of its texture or the vibratory rate of the atoms composing it.

Among these several bodies there are but the three of the coarsest texture we need to consider here, and they are the physical, astral and thought bodies.

Each of these bodies resemble the other in shape, form, general appearance, etc., their difference being largely confined to the rate at which their atoms vibrate.

Each body has its own brain, which corresponds to the physical brain, through which its mind manifests.

The will power is a faculty possessed by the mind of each of these bodies.

Just as the human mind and its will power controls man's use of Energy and its manifestations here in the material world, so does the astral mind and its

will power control them on the astral or
soul plane, and the thought mind and
its will power control them on the
thought or spiritual plane.

Each of these planes interpenetrates
the other and colors the thoughts and
acts of each mind and body according to
the receptivity of each.

The interpenetration of matter, the
occupying of the same space by two or
more material substances *of different
density*, is the fourth dimension of space.

The human mind, through which its
will power acts, is composed of the essence
emanating from the intelligence of all
the cells of the physical body.

The astral and thought minds are
formed in the same manner.

Each of these minds act and react upon
each other according to the degree of

their harmonious or inharmonious relationship with each other.

The will power is the connecting link between thoughts, ideas, images, and their materialization. Between the abstract and the concrete; between faith and facts; between the Individuality and the Personality; between the Infinite and the finite; between God and man.

Man cognizes the abstract, that is faith, God, the Infinite, the Individuality, through his astral and thought minds, his soul and spiritual states of consciousness.

Man cognizes the concrete, that is material facts, human man, the finite, the Personality, through his human mind manifesting through his physical brain.

Man's " Personality " is the essence of the consciousness stamped upon the atoms of his body by his parents, plus that absorbed from the " Individuality "which incarnates therein, plus that obtained from the experiences gained in this incarnation.

Questions for Tenth Lesson

1. What is the most important thing to you in this Lesson?
2. What is meant by the difference between the *oneness of all life* and the *oneness of all manifestations* of life?
3. What is the final goal of all vibrations emanating from each life?
4. What is a " dreamer? "
5. What is a " worshiper? "
6. What is the difference between living on one's ideals, and living for one's idols?
7. Why should we hold the thought and affirm " All is good? "
8. What do affirmations symbolize?
9. What kind of an affirmation should we always use?
10. What should we always do before making an affirmation, and why?

CONCENTRATION AND WILL POWER

by F. W. SEARS, M.P.

Eleventh Lesson

Man's " Individuality " is composed of the astral and other bodies of still finer material which come and take possession of the physical body at its birth and leave it at the period called death.

It is the function of the will power of the human mind to determine what shall be done with the multitude of thoughts, ideas, images, visions which are forever knocking at its door and seeking entrance to our human consciousness.

Shall they be allowed to enter, persist, and so materialize in form or shall the inhibiting fibers of the human brain be

165

so trained by the will power to discrimi-
nate between them, allowing some to
enter and persist until they are materialized and others to be shut out because
they are not what we want?

This is the real function of the will
power when properly trained for its work.

The will power of each mind and body
acts only for its particular mind, but such
action always reacts in some degree upon
the other minds and bodies according to
their receptivity.

The astral mind and its will power does
not always follow the lead of the human
mind and its will power, nor vice versa.

It is because of this fact and its reaction that inharmony is created between
the two nervous systems of the physical
body, the cerebro-spinal and the solar
plexus or sympathetic nervous system,

the effect of which is to produce disease in the physical body, lack in the environment, or both.

The process or action of the will power is the same for each mind in the different bodies.

In this process or action there are three separate, definite and distinct stages:

First: We have the thought, idea, image or vision.

Second: The exercise of the will power to execute or carry out into materialization the thought, idea, image or vision.

Third: The action necessary to carry out into execution the thought, idea, image, vision.

Thus for instance suppose we want a certain book on the table, we first have the thought, idea, image or vision of the book; second, we will get the book:

third, in response to our thought and willing our hand reaches out and performs the action necessary to obtain the book.

This is the process by which every action becomes the effect of the positive or negative use of the will power, no matter whether the thought, idea, image or vision is of some concrete or material thing or of some thing purely abstract and immaterial.

In the case of some abstract or immaterial thing our thought then becomes to us on the unseen side of life what our hand is on the seen side.

We might have the thought, idea, image or vision of what we wanted and hold it in our human mind all of our life without ever materializing it unless we followed it with the will to do and then the action of doing.

In the case of an abstract thing the action taken is with the thought of *realizing in our consciousness our oneness now* with what we want.

The reason we fail to materialize that which we only wish or hope for is, first because we doubt our ability to attain our desire, and second, do not follow the thought, idea, image or vision with the will to do, and then the material action or thought realization of doing.

The will power of such persons is weak and irregular in its action and until it is strengthened by constructive training and use they will continue to fail in manifesting that for which they only " hope " or " wish."

It is always important to know and understand the plane of consciousness from which our thoughts, ideals, images and visions come.

They are more limited from the physical and mental planes (these are the two planes of consciousness which are essentially human) and grow bigger and less limited on each succeeding plane.

We want to remember that *consciousness and thought habit* underlies, tinctures and colors every thought and its resultant action.

Thought habits are formed by the thoughts, ideas, images and visions which come to us and which we allow to persist, no matter whether we do this consciously or unconsciously.

Consciousness is formed by the *character* of the *thought habits* we create.

Ideas, thoughts, images, visions, have definite sensory centers in each brain whether it is the brain of the physical, astral or thought body.

Habits are memories of sensation in the brain and cells of each body caused by action being repeated many times.

Concrete habits are the result of thought habits which are expressed in material form through repeated physical action.

Abstract habits are the result of thought habits which have not yet been expressed in material form and are therefore only in our imagination, i.e., the first step only in the process of their materialization has been taken, the other two steps, willing and action, not having been performed.

One thought does not make a habit.

Neither does one affirmation change an

old thought habit nor its materialized effects.

It requires the continued and persistent thinking of the *same character of thoughts* —not necessarily the same thought— to form a new thought habit.

This is where the exercise of our will power comes in.

As an illustration of this let us take anything which is characteristic of one, such as impulsiveness, deliberation, grouch, surliness, happy, joyful, etc.

These characteristics have been formed as the result of repeating such thoughts and feeling such emotions myriads of times in this and in former incarnations.

There may have been thousands of different objects or incidents in our life which brought out the thoughts and emotions back of these characteristics but they were all of the same character and tended to produce the habit of impulsiveness or deliberation, grouch or joy, surliness or happiness.

Frequently we say " I can't help it because it is *natural* to me."

This simply means that it has become such a *fixed habit* in our life and is so much a part of us that we really believe it to be unchangeable.

The fact is however that, not knowing it is in our power to change the habit, we do not *will* to change it, and so we go on in our old habit and make it that much stronger, more fixed and more difficult to change.

" I'll try," is another pernicious and insidious thought habit we ignorantly and unconsciously get into under the belief it is a good habit to have.

It shows a weakness in the exercise of one's will power which invariably makes for failure.

When a person says " I'll try," he starts out handicapped with the consciousness of unbelief in himself and the power to do, otherwise he would say "I will," rather than " I'll try."

When one is asked to go somewhere and says " I'll try to come," you can always be assured he will not get there nine times out of ten and unconsciously says " I'll try " because he is too weak-willed to say " no."

All of our expressions and manifestations are the result of habits already formed or in the process of formation, and our will power is the arbiter of these habits.

A man spent considerable money once

in investigating a business proposition and upon finding it had been misrepresented to him and his money lost, he threatened to sue the parties and send them to prison.

He did not realize he had related with this proposition as the result of his own inharmonious consciousness which had been formed from his inharmonious thought habits resulting from his inharmonious thoughts of anger, hatred, worry, fear, anxiety, condemnation, resentment, resistance, envy, jealousy, or similar thought emotions, which his will power had permitted to enter and persist.

He did not realize that he was continuing to perpetuate these same effects in his life by continuing his same old thought habits.

When his attention was called to this he said he " Would not have his combative spirit to fight for his rights taken away."

Let me say right here that the Sears Philosophy *teaches* the Universal Laws and their application.

It does not in any way insist on any student *applying* them. That is for the student to determine for himself and we are perfectly willing for any student to go on in his old destructive thought habits and consciousness and destroy or weaken his will power just as long as he wants to do so. That is his business and we never make it ours.

It is because of this continued resentment and resistance in man's consciousness, such as this man had, that we fail to realize the weakening of our will power by our inharmonious consciousness and that our continuance of these thought habits only keep us related with such experiences again and again.

Habits and characteristics are formed unconsciously and ignorantly by most persons simply because they do not learn how to use the Universal Laws in a conscious, intelligent, constructive and harmonious way.

It is true that frequently man applies these laws consciously and intelligently along some lines but most persons fail to learn the great lesson which is that the laws they are using in forming the habit of doing certain things are Universal Laws and so are applicable to *all things*.

As a concrete illustration of this truth with which everyone is more or less familiar let us take the forming of the habit of playing on the piano.

We first place the musical scale before us.

That is the thought, idea, image or vision.

Then we will to strike certain notes on the instrument.

This is followed by our striking the notes.

When this is done only a few times or even a hundred or a thousand times we do not form the habit of striking the right key for each note every time, but when we keep on doing this—practicing as we call it—hours each day, for days, weeks, months and even years, we train the intelligence in the cells of our fingers to quickly respond to the idea, thought, image, vision, and in time the habit becomes so fixed in their cell consciousness that they do the work automatically and we can then put our human mind on something else—talk to some one for instance—while the intelligence in our fingers goes on playing the music according to the habit we have consciously taught them.

We will them to do this—set them going according to the way we have trained them—then permit them to follow the habit we have consciously taught them.

In the forming of any habit it is the thought, idea, image, vision, (whether it is a conscious one or not), which precedes the will and action that determines the kind of habit which is formed.

Questions for Eleventh Lesson

1. What is the most important thing to you in this Lesson?
2. What is the will power?
3. What is the function of the will power?
4. What effect does the will power of each body have upon the others?
5. What is the difference between one's " Personality " and " Individuality? "
6. What creates inharmony between the two nervous systems of the physical body, and what is the effect of such inharmony?
7. What is the process of the action of the will power?
8. Why do we often fail to materialize that for which we wish or hope?
9. How do we form our *consciousness and thought habits*?
10. What is the difference between abstract and concrete thought habits?

CONCENTRATION AND WILL POWER

by F. W. Sears, M.P.

Twelfth Lesson

Destructive habits are unconsciously formed through our will power becoming so weak that it fails to put a harmonious and constructive thought, idea, image or vision before our human mind and hold it there every time a destructive one comes and attempts to enter.

I once knew a man who thought it was funny and smart to always say the opposite of what he really thought and meant.

The result was that he unconsciously formed the habit of saying and doing the wrong thing at the most inopportune times.

There came a crisis in this man's life where he said and did the wrong thing with the result that he suffered great misery and a heavy financial loss.

He learned the lesson it taught him but did so at the expense of his reputation when, **had** he only used his faculties intelligently and harmoniously to have formed the right thought habit and will power, he could have saved himself all the misery, pain, suffering and financial loss he experienced.

Should the power of the human will to act be taken away either through the impairment of the physical brain, through hypnotism, or obsession, man would be without human intelligence and respond only to the instinctive or physical plane of consciousness. In other words he would return to the state **of primitive man.**

Take the case of a man who drinks. The ordinary man who uses liquor can " either drink or let it alone," when he first begins to use it; but slowly and so subtlely that he does not realize it is his power to will to *not* take a drink taken away from him through the habit he forms of continuing to drink.

His will power becomes so weakened through his failure to exercise it in *not* taking a drink that it fails to respond when he really wants to say " no."

The same is true of the man who allows himself to get angry, irritated, annoyed, or the one who permits himself to say mean, hateful things, or who criticises, condemns and judges people and things, or who forms the habit of interpretating others destructively.

The next time you have the opportun-

ity of listening to the conversation of anyone just make a note of the negative,
destructive, and inharmonious things
they say.

Look over the news in the daily papers
and observe the same thing there.

It is astonishing how this habit of
making destructive statements permeates
the world until it seems almost impossible
for two persons to hold any kind of a
conversation without indulging in it.

The tragic side of the matter is that
they do not know they are doing a
destructive thing even when their attention is called to it.

It is true that the world realizes in a
general way that anger, hatred, worry,
fear, envy, jealousy, strife and kindred
thoughts are destructive, but this realization only covers the objective action;

as long as the world only thinks or talks
these things and does not act them it
believes it is living a " good " life.

It has not yet come into the realization
that to even think or talk such thoughts
creates a consciousness of inharmony
which is destructive, aids in weakening
the will power, and in time results in
the formation of habits which are most
destructive.

Many strong wills have been made
weak through unconsciously forming
such habits.

Through conscious ideation—that is
by doing it " on purpose "—a weak will
may be made strong by persistently
repeating powerful affirmations, relaxing
and becoming receptive to their vibrations; bringing the mind back to the
affirmations again and again whenever

it strays away, but doing this without irritation, annoyance, worry or anxiety.

The making of these affirmations many times under these conditions is necessary so that their memory will form new *fixed thought habits* and so establish new relationships through them.

Strong wills are made weak through the reversal of this process.

The world has no realization whatever of the many negative affirmations it unconsciously makes during the course of a day.

A woman was attending a religious service once and lost her hand-bag with " lots of money in it."

She " didn't think anyone who came to such a place would steal," so she said.

She never realized that it would have been just as easy for her to think that she was too harmonious to lose her hand-bag, and so build that kind of a consciousness and thought habit.

Had she trained her will power to fill her thought world with only harmonious and constructive thoughts she never could have lost her hand-bag nor the money that was in it.

The *character* of her thought showed that she was dependent upon some one or some thing outside of herself for protection.

As long as we fail to recognize that everything which comes to us is the effect of causes we set in motion by the use we make of Energy through our human mind, and that the will power is the controlling power of our human mind, just so long will we go on setting causes in motion which will bring us disastrous results.

The reason many persons fail to " make good " their affirmations is because they do not use their will power to live them.

They seem to think all that is necessary is for them to affirm and that they can go on in their old way of living and the affirmations will do the work.

The world is filled with persons who do not know whether what they do is the " right " thing for them to do or not.

They must have someone else's opinion in the matter before they feel they are " right."

Their will power is in such a weakened condition that they do not have any standards of their own but govern themselves entirely by what others may say and think or do.

The result is that such persons never

know where they are at and neither does anyone else.

It is no wonder they are invariably failures for they are swayed first one way and then another by the will power of someone else.

A New York City newspaper was conducting a campaign against prizefighting once and asked two ministers of Christian churches to attend a fight and report their impressions of it to the paper, and also to preach sermons against such fights.

Before either one of these two ministers dared to attend the fight or decide whether or not to go, they had to consult with prominent members of their congregation and obtain their sanction.

Any man whose will power was so weak and wobbly that it had to be propped up by someone else, and especially a minister of the gospel who by reason of his special training, development and unfoldment is credited with greater and better standards of morality than is the ordinary mortal, who has to obtain the opinion of a layman before deciding his action in such a case, has certainly too limited a standard of morality and too weak and impotent a will power to be a safe guide even in this life, let alone for the life beyond.

There is only one salvation for a person with such a weak will power and that is for him not to do anything until he is convinced that the thing he is about to do *is* the " right " thing for him to do no matter how " wrong " a thing it might be for some one else.

We should always remember that God

—the great Universal Law—wants us to do whatever *we* want to do, for only by *expressing our wants* will we ever learn how to make our expression constructive and harmonious.

Our will power should be strong enough and yet flexible enough for us to express our wants *knowing* that whatever we do —no matter what it may be nor how disastrous in its effects—is the right thing for us to do in our present state of unfoldment, and that in accordance with the way we take the consequences and harmoniously adjust ourselves to the effects will we learn the lesson it teaches, profit by the experience, strengthen our will power, and increase our understanding of the universal laws.

One of the lessons we finally learn under such conditions is not to want to

be destructive in any way—not to con-
demn, criticise, resent, resist; not even
to regret or be sorry for anything, because
all of these thoughts and emotions are
destructive and help to weaken the
will power, but rather to be glad for our
experience because we know we have
learned our lesson from it and so it was
worth the price we had to pay in the
learning.

This does not take away from us the
privilege of analyzing either people or
things.

This we not only have the right to do
but it is necessary for us to do in order
that we may develop a deeper understanding of life, but we should not pass
judgment on them as to whether they
are "right" or "wrong" for that is
criticism.

Remember always that analysis is criticism with the sting of condemnation extracted.

It is the little things of life—not the big things—which make one's will power strong or weak in accordance with our attitude toward them.

Obstinacy and stubbornness are evidences of a weak will power, for one who will not change his attitude when he knows it is destructive demonstrates his lack of will power.

When one depends upon others for advice or assistance of any kind it is an evidence of weak will-power, and the longer one continues to do this the weaker becomes his will power.

It requires the strongest kind of a will power for one to live true to his ideals in the face of the world's condemnation and criticism, or the hostility of one's family and friends.

A case came under my notice where the wife of one of my students was continually nagging her husband because he was studying this Philosophy and doing his best to live it each day.

" You used to make money before you got mixed up with that foolishness," she told him one day.

"Yes," he replied, "and I lost it all again and was in the very depths of a hell of poverty and despair when I began to study and apply these truths.

" They saved me from suicide and are making life worth living these days and as I am learning to apply them more perfectly the more am I getting back my old strength, courage and will power but without its weakness of *force.* "

" I know now that through my *forceful efforts* I destroyed the real power of my will and I do not intend to make the same mistake again."

This man remained true to his ideals with the result that he rebuilt his fortunes and became very successful in every way.

To have a strong will power does not mean that we must *force* things.

To use *force*, either physical or mental, is an evidence of an " iron will," and just as the metal iron rusts, becomes weak and decayed, so does iron in the will power of an " iron will " rust, become weak and finally destroys itself through its own *force*.

One with a really strong will power never uses his power to *make* others do his bidding, neither does he allow others to control him.

Such a person is always kind and considerate, yet strong and powerful, no matter how great the pressure on him may become.

The strong will power is always flexible. It bends and gives a little under great pressure but never gives way nor breaks, simply because it does not resist.

Architects have recognized the value of this Law of Non-resistance in the construction of bridges and high buildings.

The Woolworth tower, the tallest building in the world, is so constructed as to give several inches under strong wind pressure and thus avoid the possibility of being blown down and destroyed by the strongest wind which it is likely to encounter.

Every one can develop a strong will power through constant training of the mind by bringing it back again and again to whatever it desires to concentrate upon; doing this quietly, calmly, without irritation, censure, worry or annoyance, and then through the harmonious and constructive use of the will power set new causes in motion which will enable one to *rise above* the effects of all our inharmonious past.

Thoughts, ideas, images and visions originate from two different sources: The finite or objective world, and the infinite or invisible world.

They come to us tinctured with the vibrations of the different planes of consciousness through which they pass; the physical, mental, soul and spiritual, and we receive and interpret them according to our development and unfoldment.

The universal Energy which materializes in form as health or disease, wealth
or poverty, love or hate, joy or sorrow,
happiness or misery, courage or fear,
harmony or inharmony, is all one and
the same Energy.

The use we make of it—the plane of
consciousness from which it comes as
well as that from which we use it—determines its effect upon our life, in our
body and environment, and it is the will
power which has the final say as to how
we will use it.

It is the will power that determines the
source from which we shall receive our
ideas, thoughts, images, visions, and it
is the will power which determines
whether or not they shall persist with us
after we have received them.

As all habits, all voluntary or automatic action depends first upon the thought, idea, image or vision we can readily see how vastly important is the training of our will power so that it will relate only with the highest, best and greatest source from which to draw our thoughts, ideas, images and visions to the end that only the most harmonious, constructive and unlimited effects may follow.

When this is accomplished there will be nothing impossible to the consciousness of man.

Questions for Twelfth Lesson

1. What is the most important thing to you in this Lesson?
2. How are constructive habits consciously formed?
3. How does our will power become weak, and how can a weak will power become strong and powerful?
4. Why is it necessary to make affirmations many times?
5. Why do some persons fail to " make good " their affirmations?
6. How do we determine what is the " right " thing for us to do?
7. What is it that makes our will power strong or weak?
8. Upon whom should one depend for advice?
9. Is an " iron will " a strong or weak will, and why?
10. What is the important thing in training the mind to develop a strong, constructive and harmonious will power?
11. How much have you been benefited in a general way from this course of lessons?
12. How much in any special way?

www.ingramcontent.com/pod-product-compliance
Lightning Source LLC
Chambersburg PA
CBHW080528090426
42733CB00015B/2517